50 Christmas Baking Recipes for Home

By: Kelly Johnson

Table of Contents

- Gingerbread Cookies
- Sugar Cookies
- Chocolate Peppermint Bark
- Snickerdoodles
- Pumpkin Pie Bars
- Eggnog Muffins
- Pecan Pie Bars
- Cranberry Orange Bread
- Holiday Biscotti
- Chocolate Crinkle Cookies
- Linzer Cookies
- White Chocolate Cranberry Cookies
- Candy Cane Brownies
- Shortbread Cookies
- Chocolate Stollen
- Almond Crescent Cookies
- Rum Balls
- Coconut Macaroons
- Fruitcake Cookies
- Chocolate Yule Log
- Gingerbread Cake
- Apple Cinnamon Muffins
- Peppermint Fudge
- Oatmeal Raisin Cookies
- Walnut Caramel Bars
- Lemon Bars
- Mocha Cookies
- Red Velvet Cake Balls
- Salted Caramel Brownies
- Hazelnut Chocolate Truffles
- Maple Pecan Cookies
- Butterscotch Blondies
- Nutmeg Spice Cake
- Cinnamon Roll Cookies
- Raspberry Almond Thumbprints
- Gingerbread Whoopie Pies

- Poppy Seed Bread
- Peppermint Hot Chocolate Cookies
- Chewy Molasses Cookies
- Cranberry Almond Granola Bars
- Chocolate Chip Pretzel Cookies
- Bourbon Balls
- Sweet Potato Pie Bars
- Chocolate Dipped Pretzels
- Carrot Cake Cupcakes
- Almond Joy Bars
- Sticky Toffee Pudding Cake
- Peanut Butter Blossoms
- Chocolate Chip Peppermint Cookies
- Christmas Stollen

Gingerbread Cookies

Ingredients:

- 3 1/4 cups all-purpose flour
- 1/2 teaspoon baking soda
- 1 tablespoon ground ginger
- 1 tablespoon ground cinnamon
- 1/2 teaspoon ground cloves
- 1/2 teaspoon salt
- 1/2 cup unsalted butter, room temperature
- 1/2 cup packed brown sugar
- 1/2 cup molasses
- 1 large egg
- 1 tablespoon fresh lemon juice (optional)

Instructions:

1. **Preheat Oven**: Preheat your oven to 350°F (175°C). Line baking sheets with parchment paper.
2. **Mix Dry Ingredients**: In a medium bowl, whisk together flour, baking soda, ginger, cinnamon, cloves, and salt.
3. **Cream Butter and Sugar**: In a large bowl, beat the butter and brown sugar until light and fluffy. Mix in the molasses, egg, and lemon juice (if using).
4. **Combine**: Gradually add the dry ingredients to the butter mixture, mixing until combined. The dough will be stiff.
5. **Roll Out Dough**: Divide the dough in half. Roll out each half on a floured surface to about 1/4-inch thickness. Cut out shapes using cookie cutters.
6. **Bake**: Place the cut-out cookies onto the prepared baking sheets. Bake for 8-10 minutes, or until the edges are firm. The centers may still be soft.
7. **Cool**: Let the cookies cool on the baking sheets for a few minutes before transferring them to wire racks to cool completely.
8. **Decorate** (optional): Decorate with royal icing or your favorite frosting once the cookies are completely cooled.

Enjoy your gingerbread cookies!

Sugar Cookies

Ingredients:

- 2 3/4 cups all-purpose flour
- 1 1/2 teaspoons baking powder
- 1/2 teaspoon salt
- 1/2 cup unsalted butter, room temperature
- 1 1/2 cups granulated sugar
- 1 large egg
- 1 teaspoon vanilla extract
- 1/4 cup milk

Instructions:

1. **Preheat Oven**: Preheat your oven to 350°F (175°C). Line baking sheets with parchment paper.
2. **Mix Dry Ingredients**: In a medium bowl, whisk together flour, baking powder, and salt. Set aside.
3. **Cream Butter and Sugar**: In a large bowl, beat the butter and granulated sugar together until light and fluffy. This should take about 3-4 minutes.
4. **Add Egg and Vanilla**: Beat in the egg and vanilla extract until well combined.
5. **Combine Ingredients**: Gradually add the dry ingredients to the butter mixture, mixing on low speed until just combined. Then, add the milk and mix until the dough comes together.
6. **Roll Out Dough**: Divide the dough in half. Roll out one half on a floured surface to about 1/8-inch thickness. Use cookie cutters to cut out shapes.
7. **Bake**: Place the cut-out cookies onto the prepared baking sheets. Bake for 8-10 minutes, or until the edges are lightly golden.
8. **Cool**: Allow the cookies to cool on the baking sheets for a few minutes before transferring them to wire racks to cool completely.
9. **Decorate** (optional): Once cooled, you can decorate the cookies with royal icing, sprinkles, or your favorite frosting.

Enjoy your delicious sugar cookies!

Chocolate Peppermint Bark

Ingredients:

- 12 ounces semisweet chocolate (chopped or chips)
- 12 ounces white chocolate (chopped or chips)
- 1/2 teaspoon peppermint extract
- 1/2 cup crushed peppermint candies or candy canes

Instructions:

1. **Prepare Baking Sheet**: Line a baking sheet with parchment paper or a silicone baking mat.
2. **Melt Semisweet Chocolate**: In a heatproof bowl over simmering water (double boiler method) or in the microwave in 30-second intervals, melt the semisweet chocolate until smooth. Stir frequently to ensure even melting. Pour the melted chocolate onto the prepared baking sheet and spread it into an even layer with a spatula. Chill in the refrigerator for about 10 minutes to set.
3. **Melt White Chocolate**: While the semisweet chocolate is setting, melt the white chocolate using the same method (double boiler or microwave), stirring until smooth.
4. **Add Peppermint Extract**: Stir the peppermint extract into the melted white chocolate.
5. **Spread White Chocolate**: Remove the baking sheet from the refrigerator and spread the melted white chocolate evenly over the set semisweet chocolate layer.
6. **Add Peppermint**: Sprinkle the crushed peppermint candies or candy canes evenly over the top while the white chocolate is still soft.
7. **Chill**: Refrigerate the bark until fully set, about 30 minutes.
8. **Break into Pieces**: Once set, break the bark into pieces or cut into squares.

Enjoy your festive and delicious Chocolate Peppermint Bark!

Snickerdoodles

Ingredients:

- **For the Cookies:**
    - 2 3/4 cups all-purpose flour
    - 2 teaspoons cream of tartar
    - 1/2 teaspoon baking soda
    - 1/4 teaspoon salt
    - 1 cup unsalted butter, room temperature
    - 1 1/2 cups granulated sugar
    - 2 large eggs
    - 1 teaspoon vanilla extract
- **For the Cinnamon Sugar Coating:**
    - 1/4 cup granulated sugar
    - 1 tablespoon ground cinnamon

Instructions:

1. **Preheat Oven**: Preheat your oven to 350°F (175°C). Line baking sheets with parchment paper.
2. **Mix Dry Ingredients**: In a medium bowl, whisk together the flour, cream of tartar, baking soda, and salt. Set aside.
3. **Cream Butter and Sugar**: In a large bowl, beat the butter and granulated sugar together until light and fluffy, about 3-4 minutes.
4. **Add Eggs and Vanilla**: Beat in the eggs one at a time, then stir in the vanilla extract until combined.
5. **Combine Ingredients**: Gradually add the dry ingredients to the wet ingredients, mixing until just combined.
6. **Prepare Cinnamon Sugar**: In a small bowl, mix together the 1/4 cup granulated sugar and 1 tablespoon ground cinnamon.
7. **Shape Cookies**: Roll the dough into 1-inch balls, then roll each ball in the cinnamon sugar mixture to coat.
8. **Bake**: Place the coated dough balls onto the prepared baking sheets, spacing them about 2 inches apart. Bake for 10-12 minutes, or until the edges are set and the centers are still soft.
9. **Cool**: Allow the cookies to cool on the baking sheets for a few minutes before transferring them to wire racks to cool completely.

Enjoy your soft and cinnamon-sweet Snickerdoodles!

Pumpkin Pie Bars

Ingredients:

- **For the Crust:**
    - 1 1/2 cups all-purpose flour
    - 1/4 cup granulated sugar
    - 1/2 teaspoon salt
    - 1/2 cup unsalted butter, cold and cut into cubes
- **For the Pumpkin Filling:**
    - 1 (15-ounce) can pumpkin puree
    - 1 cup granulated sugar
    - 1/2 cup packed brown sugar
    - 1/2 teaspoon salt
    - 1 teaspoon ground cinnamon
    - 1/2 teaspoon ground ginger
    - 1/4 teaspoon ground cloves
    - 1/4 teaspoon ground nutmeg
    - 4 large eggs
    - 1 cup heavy cream

Instructions:

1. **Preheat Oven**: Preheat your oven to 350°F (175°C). Line a 9x13-inch baking pan with parchment paper, leaving some overhang for easy removal.
2. **Prepare the Crust**:
    - In a medium bowl, whisk together the flour, sugar, and salt.
    - Cut in the cold butter using a pastry cutter or your fingers until the mixture resembles coarse crumbs.
    - Press the mixture evenly into the bottom of the prepared baking pan.
3. **Bake the Crust**: Bake the crust in the preheated oven for 15 minutes, or until lightly golden. Remove from the oven and set aside.
4. **Prepare the Filling**:
    - In a large bowl, whisk together the pumpkin puree, granulated sugar, brown sugar, salt, cinnamon, ginger, cloves, and nutmeg until well combined.
    - Add the eggs one at a time, whisking well after each addition.
    - Gradually whisk in the heavy cream until the mixture is smooth and well combined.
5. **Assemble**:
    - Pour the pumpkin filling over the pre-baked crust and spread it evenly with a spatula.
6. **Bake**: Return the pan to the oven and bake for 40-45 minutes, or until the filling is set and the edges are slightly puffed. The center should be firm but may still have a slight jiggle.

7. **Cool**: Allow the bars to cool completely in the pan on a wire rack. Once cooled, lift the bars out of the pan using the parchment paper overhang and cut into squares.
8. **Serve**: Serve as is or with a dollop of whipped cream.

Enjoy your Pumpkin Pie Bars!

Eggnog Muffins

Ingredients:

- **For the Muffins:**
    - 2 1/2 cups all-purpose flour
    - 1 cup granulated sugar
    - 1 tablespoon baking powder
    - 1/2 teaspoon salt
    - 1/2 teaspoon ground nutmeg
    - 1/2 teaspoon ground cinnamon
    - 1/2 cup unsalted butter, melted and cooled
    - 1 cup eggnog
    - 2 large eggs
    - 1 teaspoon vanilla extract
- **For the Topping (optional):**
    - 2 tablespoons granulated sugar
    - 1/2 teaspoon ground cinnamon

Instructions:

1. **Preheat Oven**: Preheat your oven to 375°F (190°C). Line a 12-cup muffin tin with paper liners or lightly grease the cups.
2. **Mix Dry Ingredients**: In a large bowl, whisk together the flour, sugar, baking powder, salt, nutmeg, and cinnamon.
3. **Mix Wet Ingredients**: In another bowl, whisk together the melted butter, eggnog, eggs, and vanilla extract.
4. **Combine Ingredients**: Pour the wet ingredients into the dry ingredients and stir until just combined. Be careful not to overmix; the batter should be a bit lumpy.
5. **Fill Muffin Tin**: Divide the batter evenly among the 12 muffin cups, filling each about 3/4 full.
6. **Prepare Topping (optional)**: If using, mix the granulated sugar and ground cinnamon together in a small bowl. Sprinkle the mixture evenly over the muffin batter.
7. **Bake**: Bake for 18-22 minutes, or until a toothpick inserted into the center of a muffin comes out clean.
8. **Cool**: Allow the muffins to cool in the tin for about 5 minutes, then transfer them to a wire rack to cool completely.

Enjoy your delicious Eggnog Muffins!

Pecan Pie Bars

Ingredients:

- **For the Crust:**
    - 1 3/4 cups all-purpose flour
    - 1/4 cup granulated sugar
    - 1/2 teaspoon salt
    - 1/2 cup unsalted butter, cold and cut into cubes
- **For the Filling:**
    - 1 cup light brown sugar, packed
    - 1/2 cup corn syrup (light or dark)
    - 1/4 cup unsalted butter, melted
    - 3 large eggs
    - 1 1/2 teaspoons vanilla extract
    - 1/4 teaspoon salt
    - 1 1/2 cups pecan halves

Instructions:

1. **Preheat Oven**: Preheat your oven to 350°F (175°C). Line a 9x13-inch baking pan with parchment paper, leaving some overhang for easy removal.
2. **Prepare the Crust**:
    - In a medium bowl, whisk together the flour, sugar, and salt.
    - Cut in the cold butter using a pastry cutter or your fingers until the mixture resembles coarse crumbs.
    - Press the mixture evenly into the bottom of the prepared baking pan.
3. **Bake the Crust**: Bake the crust in the preheated oven for 12-15 minutes, or until lightly golden. Remove from the oven and set aside.
4. **Prepare the Filling**:
    - In a large bowl, whisk together the brown sugar, corn syrup, melted butter, eggs, vanilla extract, and salt until smooth and well combined.
    - Stir in the pecan halves until evenly distributed.
5. **Assemble**:
    - Pour the pecan filling over the pre-baked crust, spreading it evenly.
6. **Bake**: Return the pan to the oven and bake for 30-35 minutes, or until the filling is set and the top is golden brown.
7. **Cool**: Allow the bars to cool completely in the pan on a wire rack. Once cooled, lift the bars out of the pan using the parchment paper overhang and cut into squares.

Enjoy your delicious Pecan Pie Bars!

Cranberry Orange Bread

Ingredients:

- **For the Bread:**
    - 2 cups all-purpose flour
    - 1 cup granulated sugar
    - 1/2 teaspoon baking powder
    - 1/2 teaspoon baking soda
    - 1/2 teaspoon salt
    - 1/2 teaspoon ground cinnamon
    - 1/4 teaspoon ground nutmeg
    - 1/2 cup unsalted butter, melted and cooled
    - 1/2 cup orange juice (freshly squeezed is best)
    - 2 large eggs
    - 1 tablespoon orange zest
    - 1 1/2 cups fresh or frozen cranberries (coarsely chopped if large)
- **For the Glaze (optional):**
    - 1/2 cup powdered sugar
    - 1-2 tablespoons orange juice

Instructions:

1. **Preheat Oven**: Preheat your oven to 350°F (175°C). Grease and flour a 9x5-inch loaf pan or line it with parchment paper.
2. **Mix Dry Ingredients**: In a large bowl, whisk together the flour, sugar, baking powder, baking soda, salt, cinnamon, and nutmeg.
3. **Mix Wet Ingredients**: In another bowl, whisk together the melted butter, orange juice, eggs, and orange zest until well combined.
4. **Combine Ingredients**: Pour the wet ingredients into the dry ingredients and stir until just combined. Fold in the cranberries. Be careful not to overmix; the batter should be lumpy.
5. **Pour Batter**: Pour the batter into the prepared loaf pan and spread it evenly.
6. **Bake**: Bake for 55-65 minutes, or until a toothpick inserted into the center of the bread comes out clean. The top should be golden brown.
7. **Cool**: Allow the bread to cool in the pan for about 10 minutes before transferring it to a wire rack to cool completely.
8. **Prepare Glaze (optional)**: If using the glaze, whisk together the powdered sugar and orange juice until smooth. Drizzle over the cooled bread.

Enjoy your Cranberry Orange Bread!

Holiday Biscotti

Ingredients:

- **For the Biscotti:**
    - 2 1/4 cups all-purpose flour
    - 1 cup granulated sugar
    - 1/2 teaspoon baking powder
    - 1/2 teaspoon baking soda
    - 1/4 teaspoon salt
    - 1/2 cup unsalted butter, softened
    - 2 large eggs
    - 1 teaspoon vanilla extract
    - 1 teaspoon almond extract
    - 1 cup dried cranberries
    - 1/2 cup chopped nuts (such as pistachios, walnuts, or almonds)
    - 1/2 cup white chocolate chips (optional)
- **For the Glaze (optional):**
    - 1/2 cup powdered sugar
    - 1-2 tablespoons milk or water

Instructions:

1. **Preheat Oven**: Preheat your oven to 350°F (175°C). Line a baking sheet with parchment paper or a silicone baking mat.
2. **Mix Dry Ingredients**: In a medium bowl, whisk together the flour, sugar, baking powder, baking soda, and salt.
3. **Cream Butter and Eggs**: In a large bowl, beat the softened butter until creamy. Add the eggs one at a time, beating well after each addition. Mix in the vanilla extract and almond extract.
4. **Combine Ingredients**: Gradually add the dry ingredients to the butter mixture, mixing until just combined. Stir in the dried cranberries, chopped nuts, and white chocolate chips (if using).
5. **Shape Dough**: Divide the dough in half and shape each portion into a log about 12 inches long and 2 inches wide. Place the logs on the prepared baking sheet, spacing them about 3 inches apart.
6. **Bake**: Bake for 25-30 minutes, or until the logs are golden brown and firm to the touch. Allow them to cool on the baking sheet for about 10 minutes.
7. **Slice Logs**: Using a serrated knife, carefully slice the logs diagonally into 1/2-inch wide pieces.
8. **Second Bake**: Arrange the biscotti slices cut side down on the baking sheet. Bake for an additional 10-15 minutes, or until they are crisp and golden.
9. **Cool**: Allow the biscotti to cool completely on a wire rack.
10. **Prepare Glaze (optional)**: If using, whisk together the powdered sugar and milk or water until smooth. Drizzle the glaze over the cooled biscotti.

Enjoy your festive Holiday Biscotti!

Chocolate Crinkle Cookies

Ingredients:

- **For the Cookies:**
    - 1/2 cup (1 stick) unsalted butter, softened
    - 1 cup granulated sugar
    - 1/2 cup unsweetened cocoa powder
    - 1/4 teaspoon salt
    - 1/2 teaspoon baking powder
    - 2 large eggs
    - 1 teaspoon vanilla extract
    - 1 1/2 cups all-purpose flour
- **For Rolling:**
    - 1/2 cup granulated sugar
    - 1/2 cup powdered sugar

Instructions:

1. **Preheat Oven**: Preheat your oven to 350°F (175°C). Line baking sheets with parchment paper or silicone baking mats.
2. **Mix Dry Ingredients**: In a small bowl, whisk together the cocoa powder, flour, salt, and baking powder. Set aside.
3. **Cream Butter and Sugar**: In a large bowl, beat the softened butter and granulated sugar together until light and fluffy.
4. **Add Eggs and Vanilla**: Beat in the eggs one at a time, then stir in the vanilla extract.
5. **Combine Ingredients**: Gradually add the dry ingredients to the butter mixture, mixing until just combined.
6. **Chill Dough**: Refrigerate the dough for about 30 minutes to make it easier to handle.
7. **Prepare Rolling Coatings**: In separate bowls, place the granulated sugar and powdered sugar.
8. **Form Cookies**: Roll the chilled dough into 1-inch balls. Roll each ball in the granulated sugar, then in the powdered sugar, coating generously.
9. **Bake**: Place the coated dough balls on the prepared baking sheets, spacing them about 2 inches apart. Bake for 10-12 minutes, or until the edges are set and the tops are cracked.
10. **Cool**: Allow the cookies to cool on the baking sheets for a few minutes before transferring them to wire racks to cool completely.

Enjoy your Chocolate Crinkle Cookies!

Linzer Cookies

Ingredients:

- **For the Dough:**
    - 2 1/2 cups all-purpose flour
    - 1/2 teaspoon baking powder
    - 1/4 teaspoon salt
    - 1 cup unsalted butter, softened
    - 1/2 cup granulated sugar
    - 1/2 cup packed brown sugar
    - 1 large egg
    - 1 teaspoon vanilla extract
    - 1/2 cup finely ground almonds (or almond meal)
- **For Filling:**
    - 1/2 cup raspberry or apricot jam (or your preferred fruit jam)
- **For Dusting:**
    - Powdered sugar, for dusting

Instructions:

1. **Preheat Oven**: Preheat your oven to 350°F (175°C). Line baking sheets with parchment paper.
2. **Mix Dry Ingredients**: In a medium bowl, whisk together the flour, baking powder, and salt. Set aside.
3. **Cream Butter and Sugars**: In a large bowl, beat the butter, granulated sugar, and brown sugar together until light and fluffy.
4. **Add Egg and Vanilla**: Beat in the egg and vanilla extract until well combined.
5. **Combine Ingredients**: Gradually add the dry ingredients to the butter mixture, mixing until just combined. Stir in the ground almonds.
6. **Chill Dough**: Divide the dough in half, wrap in plastic wrap, and refrigerate for at least 1 hour, or until firm.
7. **Roll Out Dough**: On a lightly floured surface, roll out one portion of the dough to about 1/8-inch thickness. Cut out shapes using cookie cutters. If making Linzer cookies, cut out centers from half of the cookies using a smaller cutter or a decorative shape.
8. **Bake**: Place the cookies on the prepared baking sheets. Bake for 10-12 minutes, or until the edges are lightly golden.
9. **Cool**: Allow the cookies to cool completely on a wire rack.
10. **Assemble Cookies**: Spread a small amount of jam on the flat side of each whole cookie. Place a cut-out cookie on top of the jam to create a sandwich. Dust with powdered sugar before serving.

Enjoy your beautiful and delicious Linzer Cookies!

White Chocolate Cranberry Cookies

Ingredients:

- **For the Cookies:**
    - 1 1/2 cups all-purpose flour
    - 1/2 teaspoon baking powder
    - 1/2 teaspoon baking soda
    - 1/4 teaspoon salt
    - 1/2 cup unsalted butter, softened
    - 1/2 cup granulated sugar
    - 1/2 cup packed brown sugar
    - 1 large egg
    - 1 teaspoon vanilla extract
    - 1 cup white chocolate chips
    - 1 cup dried cranberries (coarsely chopped if large)

Instructions:

1. **Preheat Oven**: Preheat your oven to 350°F (175°C). Line baking sheets with parchment paper or silicone baking mats.
2. **Mix Dry Ingredients**: In a medium bowl, whisk together the flour, baking powder, baking soda, and salt. Set aside.
3. **Cream Butter and Sugars**: In a large bowl, beat the softened butter, granulated sugar, and brown sugar together until light and fluffy.
4. **Add Egg and Vanilla**: Beat in the egg and vanilla extract until well combined.
5. **Combine Ingredients**: Gradually add the dry ingredients to the butter mixture, mixing until just combined. Fold in the white chocolate chips and dried cranberries.
6. **Form Cookies**: Drop rounded tablespoons of dough onto the prepared baking sheets, spacing them about 2 inches apart.
7. **Bake**: Bake for 10-12 minutes, or until the edges are lightly golden and the centers are set.
8. **Cool**: Allow the cookies to cool on the baking sheets for a few minutes before transferring them to wire racks to cool completely.

Enjoy your delicious White Chocolate Cranberry Cookies!

Candy Cane Brownies

Ingredients:

- **For the Brownies:**
    - 1/2 cup (1 stick) unsalted butter
    - 1 cup granulated sugar
    - 2 large eggs
    - 1 teaspoon vanilla extract
    - 1/3 cup unsweetened cocoa powder
    - 1/2 cup all-purpose flour
    - 1/4 teaspoon salt
    - 1/4 teaspoon baking powder
    - 1/2 cup mini chocolate chips (optional)
- **For the Topping:**
    - 1/2 cup white chocolate chips or chopped white chocolate
    - 1/4 cup crushed candy canes (about 5-6 candy canes)

Instructions:

1. **Preheat Oven**: Preheat your oven to 350°F (175°C). Grease and flour an 8x8-inch baking pan, or line it with parchment paper.
2. **Prepare Brownie Batter**:
    - In a medium saucepan, melt the butter over low heat. Remove from heat and stir in the sugar, eggs, and vanilla extract.
    - Beat in the cocoa powder, flour, salt, and baking powder until well combined.
    - If using, fold in the mini chocolate chips.
3. **Bake Brownies**: Pour the batter into the prepared baking pan and spread it evenly. Bake for 20-25 minutes, or until a toothpick inserted into the center comes out with a few moist crumbs.
4. **Cool**: Allow the brownies to cool completely in the pan on a wire rack before adding the topping.
5. **Prepare Topping**:
    - Melt the white chocolate chips in a microwave-safe bowl in 20-second intervals, stirring in between, until smooth. Alternatively, you can melt the white chocolate over a double boiler.
    - Spread the melted white chocolate evenly over the cooled brownies.
6. **Add Candy Canes**: Sprinkle the crushed candy canes over the white chocolate while it is still soft.
7. **Set**: Allow the white chocolate to set completely before cutting the brownies into squares.

Enjoy your festive Candy Cane Brownies!

Shortbread Cookies

Ingredients:

- 1 cup (2 sticks) unsalted butter, softened
- 1/2 cup granulated sugar
- 1/4 cup packed brown sugar (optional, for a slightly richer flavor)
- 1/4 teaspoon salt
- 2 cups all-purpose flour
- 1 teaspoon vanilla extract (optional, for added flavor)

Instructions:

1. **Preheat Oven**: Preheat your oven to 350°F (175°C). Line baking sheets with parchment paper or silicone baking mats.
2. **Cream Butter and Sugars**: In a large bowl, beat the softened butter until creamy. Add the granulated sugar and brown sugar (if using) and beat until light and fluffy. If using, mix in the vanilla extract.
3. **Combine Dry Ingredients**: Gradually add the flour and salt to the butter mixture, mixing until just combined. The dough will be crumbly but should hold together when pressed.
4. **Shape Dough**: Turn the dough out onto a lightly floured surface and gently knead it a few times until it comes together. Roll out the dough to about 1/4-inch thickness. Cut into shapes using cookie cutters or simply cut into rectangles or squares.
5. **Chill Dough (Optional)**: For cleaner edges and easier handling, you can chill the cut-out cookies on the baking sheet in the refrigerator for about 10-15 minutes before baking.
6. **Bake**: Place the cookies on the prepared baking sheets. Bake for 12-15 minutes, or until the edges are lightly golden. The centers should remain pale.
7. **Cool**: Allow the cookies to cool on the baking sheets for a few minutes before transferring them to wire racks to cool completely.

Enjoy your buttery and delicious Shortbread Cookies!

Chocolate Stollen

Ingredients:

- **For the Dough:**
    - 1/2 cup milk
    - 1/4 cup granulated sugar
    - 2 1/4 teaspoons (1 packet) active dry yeast
    - 1/2 cup unsalted butter, softened
    - 1/4 cup packed brown sugar
    - 1 large egg
    - 3 1/2 cups all-purpose flour
    - 1/2 teaspoon salt
    - 1/2 teaspoon ground cinnamon
    - 1/4 teaspoon ground nutmeg
    - 1/2 cup finely chopped dark chocolate or chocolate chips
    - 1/2 cup chopped nuts (such as almonds or walnuts, optional)
    - 1/2 cup dried cherries or raisins (optional)
- **For the Filling:**
    - 1/2 cup marzipan (store-bought or homemade, cut into small pieces)
- **For the Glaze (optional):**
    - 2 tablespoons unsalted butter, melted
    - 1/4 cup powdered sugar
    - 1-2 tablespoons milk

Instructions:

1. **Prepare the Yeast Mixture:**
    - In a small saucepan, heat the milk until warm but not hot (about 110°F or 45°C). Stir in the granulated sugar until dissolved.
    - Sprinkle the yeast over the milk mixture and let it sit for about 5-10 minutes, or until foamy.
2. **Make the Dough:**
    - In a large bowl, combine the flour, salt, cinnamon, and nutmeg.
    - In another bowl, cream together the softened butter and brown sugar until light and fluffy. Beat in the egg.
    - Gradually add the flour mixture to the butter mixture, alternating with the yeast mixture, until a soft dough forms. Stir in the chopped chocolate, nuts, and dried cherries or raisins, if using.
3. **Knead and Rise:**
    - Turn the dough out onto a lightly floured surface and knead for about 5 minutes, or until smooth and elastic.
    - Place the dough in a lightly greased bowl, cover with a damp cloth or plastic wrap, and let it rise in a warm place for about 1-1.5 hours, or until doubled in size.
4. **Shape the Stollen:**
    - Punch down the dough and turn it out onto a lightly floured surface. Roll it into a rectangle about 1/2-inch thick.

- Spread the marzipan pieces over the dough, then roll the dough into a log. Place the log on a baking sheet lined with parchment paper.
- Shape the log into a crescent shape, if desired, and place it on the baking sheet. Cover with a cloth and let it rise for another 30 minutes.

5. **Bake**:
   - Preheat your oven to 350°F (175°C). Bake the stollen for 30-35 minutes, or until golden brown and a toothpick inserted into the center comes out clean.

6. **Cool and Glaze**:
   - Allow the stollen to cool on a wire rack.
   - If desired, brush the warm stollen with melted butter and dust with powdered sugar mixed with milk to make a glaze.

Enjoy your Chocolate Stollen, perfect for holiday gatherings or as a special treat any time of year!

Almond Crescent Cookies

Ingredients:

- **For the Cookies:**
    - 1 cup (2 sticks) unsalted butter, softened
    - 1/2 cup granulated sugar
    - 1 teaspoon vanilla extract
    - 2 cups all-purpose flour
    - 1 cup finely chopped almonds (or almond meal)
    - 1/4 teaspoon salt
- **For Rolling:**
    - 1/2 cup powdered sugar

Instructions:

1. **Preheat Oven**: Preheat your oven to 350°F (175°C). Line baking sheets with parchment paper or silicone baking mats.
2. **Cream Butter and Sugar**: In a large bowl, beat the softened butter and granulated sugar together until light and fluffy. Mix in the vanilla extract.
3. **Combine Dry Ingredients**: In another bowl, whisk together the flour, chopped almonds (or almond meal), and salt.
4. **Mix Dough**: Gradually add the dry ingredients to the butter mixture, mixing until just combined. The dough will be crumbly but should come together when pressed.
5. **Shape Cookies**: Take small portions of dough and roll them into 1-inch logs, then bend them into crescent shapes. Place them on the prepared baking sheets.
6. **Bake**: Bake for 12-15 minutes, or until the edges are lightly golden. The centers should remain pale.
7. **Cool and Coat**: Allow the cookies to cool on the baking sheets for a few minutes. While still warm, roll the cookies in powdered sugar to coat.
8. **Cool Completely**: Transfer the cookies to wire racks to cool completely.

Enjoy your delicate and nutty Almond Crescent Cookies!

Rum Balls

Ingredients:

- **For the Rum Balls:**
    - 2 cups crushed vanilla wafers (about 1 package)
    - 1 cup finely chopped nuts (such as walnuts or pecans)
    - 1 cup powdered sugar
    - 2 tablespoons unsweetened cocoa powder
    - 1/4 cup dark rum (or adjust to taste)
    - 2 tablespoons light corn syrup or honey
    - 1 teaspoon vanilla extract
- **For Rolling (optional):**
    - 1/2 cup granulated sugar
    - 1/2 cup powdered sugar
    - 1/2 cup cocoa powder

Instructions:

1. **Combine Dry Ingredients**: In a large bowl, mix together the crushed vanilla wafers, chopped nuts, powdered sugar, and cocoa powder.
2. **Add Wet Ingredients**: Add the dark rum, corn syrup (or honey), and vanilla extract to the dry mixture. Stir until everything is well combined and the mixture starts to come together.
3. **Form Balls**: Using your hands or a small cookie scoop, form the mixture into 1-inch balls and place them on a baking sheet lined with parchment paper.
4. **Chill**: Refrigerate the rum balls for at least 1 hour to firm up.
5. **Roll in Coatings (optional)**: If you like, roll the chilled rum balls in a mixture of granulated sugar, powdered sugar, and cocoa powder to coat.
6. **Store**: Keep the rum balls in an airtight container in the refrigerator. They can be enjoyed straight away but often taste even better after a day or two as the flavors meld.

Enjoy your delicious and festive Rum Balls!

Coconut Macaroons

Ingredients:

- **For the Macaroons:**
    - 4 cups sweetened shredded coconut
    - 1/2 cup granulated sugar
    - 1/4 cup all-purpose flour
    - 1/4 teaspoon salt
    - 4 large egg whites
    - 1 teaspoon vanilla extract
- **For Dipping (optional):**
    - 1/2 cup semi-sweet chocolate chips or chopped semi-sweet chocolate
    - 1 teaspoon vegetable oil (for melting the chocolate)

Instructions:

1. **Preheat Oven**: Preheat your oven to 325°F (165°C). Line a baking sheet with parchment paper or a silicone baking mat.
2. **Mix Dry Ingredients**: In a large bowl, combine the shredded coconut, granulated sugar, flour, and salt.
3. **Beat Egg Whites**: In a separate bowl, beat the egg whites with an electric mixer until stiff peaks form.
4. **Combine Ingredients**: Gently fold the beaten egg whites and vanilla extract into the coconut mixture until well combined. Be careful not to deflate the egg whites too much.
5. **Shape Macaroons**: Use a small cookie scoop or a tablespoon to drop heaping mounds of the mixture onto the prepared baking sheet. Space them about 1 inch apart.
6. **Bake**: Bake for 15-20 minutes, or until the macaroons are golden brown on the edges. The centers should remain chewy.
7. **Cool**: Allow the macaroons to cool on the baking sheet for a few minutes before transferring them to wire racks to cool completely.
8. **Optional Chocolate Dipping**:
    - Melt the chocolate chips and vegetable oil together in a microwave-safe bowl in 20-second intervals, stirring in between until smooth.
    - Dip the bottoms of the cooled macaroons into the melted chocolate and place them back on the parchment-lined baking sheet.
    - Let the chocolate set before serving.

Enjoy your delicious Coconut Macaroons, whether plain or dipped in chocolate!

Fruitcake Cookies

Ingredients:

- **For the Cookies:**
  - 1 cup unsalted butter, softened
  - 1 cup granulated sugar
  - 1/2 cup packed brown sugar
  - 2 large eggs
  - 1 teaspoon vanilla extract
  - 2 1/2 cups all-purpose flour
  - 1/2 teaspoon baking soda
  - 1/2 teaspoon baking powder
  - 1/4 teaspoon salt
  - 1 teaspoon ground cinnamon
  - 1/2 teaspoon ground nutmeg
  - 1 cup chopped mixed candied fruit
  - 1 cup chopped nuts (such as walnuts or pecans)
  - 1 cup raisins or currants

Instructions:

1. **Preheat Oven**: Preheat your oven to 350°F (175°C). Line baking sheets with parchment paper or silicone baking mats.
2. **Cream Butter and Sugars**: In a large bowl, beat the softened butter, granulated sugar, and brown sugar together until light and fluffy.
3. **Add Eggs and Vanilla**: Beat in the eggs one at a time, then mix in the vanilla extract.
4. **Mix Dry Ingredients**: In another bowl, whisk together the flour, baking soda, baking powder, salt, cinnamon, and nutmeg.
5. **Combine Ingredients**: Gradually add the dry ingredients to the butter mixture, mixing until just combined. Fold in the chopped candied fruit, nuts, and raisins or currants.
6. **Drop Cookies**: Use a cookie scoop or tablespoon to drop rounded balls of dough onto the prepared baking sheets, spacing them about 2 inches apart.
7. **Bake**: Bake for 12-15 minutes, or until the edges are lightly golden. The centers should be set but still soft.
8. **Cool**: Allow the cookies to cool on the baking sheets for a few minutes before transferring them to wire racks to cool completely.

These Fruitcake Cookies offer a festive twist on a traditional holiday treat, packed with sweet and spiced flavors! Enjoy!

Chocolate Yule Log

Ingredients:

- **For the Sponge Cake:**
    - 4 large eggs
    - 1 cup granulated sugar
    - 1/2 cup all-purpose flour
    - 1/2 cup unsweetened cocoa powder
    - 1/4 teaspoon salt
    - 1/2 teaspoon vanilla extract
- **For the Chocolate Ganache:**
    - 8 ounces semi-sweet chocolate, chopped
    - 1 cup heavy cream
    - 2 tablespoons unsalted butter
- **For the Filling (optional):**
    - 1 cup heavy cream
    - 2 tablespoons powdered sugar
    - 1 teaspoon vanilla extract
- **For Decoration (optional):**
    - Powdered sugar, for dusting
    - Fresh berries or holly (for garnish)

Instructions:

1. **Preheat Oven**: Preheat your oven to 350°F (175°C). Line a 15x10-inch jelly roll pan with parchment paper, leaving a little overhang on the sides for easy removal.
2. **Prepare the Sponge Cake**:
    - In a large bowl, beat the eggs with an electric mixer on high speed until thick and pale, about 3-4 minutes.
    - Gradually add the granulated sugar, beating until the mixture is thick and fluffy.
    - Sift together the flour, cocoa powder, and salt. Gently fold the dry ingredients into the egg mixture, being careful not to deflate the batter. Stir in the vanilla extract.
    - Pour the batter into the prepared pan and spread it evenly.
3. **Bake the Cake**: Bake for 10-12 minutes, or until the cake springs back when lightly touched.
4. **Roll the Cake**:
    - While the cake is baking, prepare a clean kitchen towel by dusting it with powdered sugar.
    - Immediately after removing the cake from the oven, turn it out onto the prepared towel. Carefully peel off the parchment paper.
    - Starting at one end, gently roll the cake up with the towel, forming a log shape. Let it cool completely while rolled up.
5. **Prepare the Ganache**:
    - In a heatproof bowl, combine the chopped chocolate and butter. Heat the heavy cream in a saucepan until just boiling, then pour it over the chocolate and butter. Let it sit for a few minutes to soften.
    - Stir the mixture until smooth and glossy. Let it cool slightly before using.
6. **Prepare the Filling (optional)**:

- In a medium bowl, whip the heavy cream, powdered sugar, and vanilla extract until stiff peaks form.
7. **Assemble the Yule Log**:
    - Unroll the cooled cake carefully and spread the filling (if using) evenly over the surface.
    - Roll the cake back up without the towel, creating a log shape. Place the cake seam-side down on a serving platter.
8. **Frost the Cake**:
    - Spread the chocolate ganache over the entire cake, smoothing it out with a spatula. Create a bark-like texture by dragging the spatula or a fork through the ganache.
9. **Decorate**:
    - Dust with powdered sugar if desired and garnish with fresh berries or holly.
10. **Chill and Serve**:
    - Refrigerate the Yule Log for at least 1 hour to set before slicing and serving.

Enjoy your elegant and delicious Chocolate Yule Log!

Gingerbread Cake

Ingredients:

- **For the Cake:**

- 2 1/2 cups all-purpose flour
- 1 1/2 teaspoons baking soda
- 1 teaspoon ground ginger
- 1 teaspoon ground cinnamon
- 1/2 teaspoon ground cloves
- 1/4 teaspoon ground nutmeg
- 1/2 teaspoon salt
- 1/2 cup (1 stick) unsalted butter, softened
- 1 cup granulated sugar
- 1/2 cup packed brown sugar
- 2 large eggs
- 1 cup molasses
- 1 cup hot water
- 1/2 cup buttermilk (or milk with 1 tablespoon lemon juice or vinegar, let sit for 5 minutes)

- **For the Optional Glaze:**
    - 1 cup powdered sugar
    - 2-3 tablespoons milk or cream
    - 1/2 teaspoon vanilla extract

Instructions:

1. **Preheat Oven**: Preheat your oven to 350°F (175°C). Grease and flour a 9x13-inch baking pan or two 8-inch round cake pans.
2. **Prepare Dry Ingredients**: In a medium bowl, whisk together the flour, baking soda, ginger, cinnamon, cloves, nutmeg, and salt. Set aside.
3. **Cream Butter and Sugars**: In a large bowl, beat the softened butter, granulated sugar, and brown sugar together until light and fluffy.
4. **Add Eggs and Molasses**: Beat in the eggs one at a time, then mix in the molasses.
5. **Combine Ingredients**: Gradually add the dry ingredients to the butter mixture, alternating with the hot water and buttermilk. Begin and end with the dry ingredients. Mix until just combined.
6. **Pour and Bake**: Pour the batter into the prepared baking pan(s). Smooth the top with a spatula.
    - For a 9x13-inch pan, bake for 35-40 minutes.
    - For 8-inch round pans, bake for 25-30 minutes.
7. Bake until a toothpick inserted into the center comes out clean or with a few moist crumbs.
8. **Cool**: Allow the cake to cool in the pan for 10 minutes before transferring to a wire rack to cool completely.
9. **Prepare the Glaze (optional)**:
    - In a small bowl, whisk together the powdered sugar, milk (or cream), and vanilla extract until smooth. Adjust the consistency with more milk if necessary.
10. **Frost and Serve**:
    - Once the cake is completely cooled, drizzle or spread the glaze over the top.

Enjoy your moist and flavorful Gingerbread Cake!

Apple Cinnamon Muffins

Ingredients:

- **For the Muffins:**
    - 1 1/2 cups all-purpose flour

- 1 cup granulated sugar
- 1 tablespoon baking powder
- 1/2 teaspoon salt
- 1 teaspoon ground cinnamon
- 1/2 teaspoon ground nutmeg
- 1/2 cup (1 stick) unsalted butter, melted
- 1/2 cup milk
- 2 large eggs
- 1 teaspoon vanilla extract
- 1 1/2 cups peeled, cored, and diced apples (about 1 medium apple)
- 1/2 cup chopped nuts (such as walnuts or pecans, optional)
- **For the Cinnamon Sugar Topping (optional):**
  - 1/4 cup granulated sugar
  - 1 teaspoon ground cinnamon
  - 2 tablespoons unsalted butter, melted

Instructions:

1. **Preheat Oven**: Preheat your oven to 375°F (190°C). Line a 12-cup muffin tin with paper liners or grease the cups.
2. **Prepare Dry Ingredients**: In a large bowl, whisk together the flour, granulated sugar, baking powder, salt, cinnamon, and nutmeg.
3. **Mix Wet Ingredients**: In another bowl, whisk together the melted butter, milk, eggs, and vanilla extract.
4. **Combine Ingredients**: Add the wet ingredients to the dry ingredients and stir until just combined. Fold in the diced apples and nuts, if using. The batter will be thick.
5. **Fill Muffin Cups**: Divide the batter evenly among the muffin cups, filling each about 3/4 full.
6. **Prepare Topping (optional)**: In a small bowl, mix together the granulated sugar and cinnamon for the topping. Brush the tops of the muffins with melted butter and sprinkle with the cinnamon sugar mixture.
7. **Bake**: Bake for 18-22 minutes, or until a toothpick inserted into the center comes out clean.
8. **Cool**: Allow the muffins to cool in the pan for 5 minutes, then transfer to a wire rack to cool completely.

Enjoy your delicious Apple Cinnamon Muffins with a hot cup of coffee or tea!

Peppermint Fudge

Ingredients:

- **For the Fudge:**
  - 2 cups granulated sugar

- 1/2 cup unsalted butter
- 2/3 cup evaporated milk
- 1 cup mini marshmallows
- 1 cup semisweet chocolate chips
- 1/2 cup crushed peppermint candies or candy canes
- 1 teaspoon vanilla extract
- **For Garnish (optional):**
  - Additional crushed peppermint candies

Instructions:

1. **Prepare Pan**: Line an 8x8-inch baking dish with parchment paper or foil, leaving an overhang for easy removal. Lightly grease the parchment paper or foil.
2. **Cook Sugar Mixture**:
   - In a medium saucepan, combine the granulated sugar, butter, and evaporated milk. Cook over medium heat, stirring constantly until the mixture reaches a full boil.
   - Continue to boil for 4-5 minutes, stirring frequently, until the mixture reaches the soft-ball stage (about 234°F to 240°F or 112°C to 115°C on a candy thermometer).
3. **Add Marshmallows and Chocolate**:
   - Remove the saucepan from heat. Stir in the mini marshmallows and chocolate chips until melted and smooth.
   - Mix in the crushed peppermint candies and vanilla extract.
4. **Pour and Cool**:
   - Pour the fudge mixture into the prepared baking dish and spread it evenly with a spatula.
   - Garnish with additional crushed peppermint candies if desired.
5. **Chill**:
   - Refrigerate the fudge for at least 2 hours, or until firm.
6. **Cut and Serve**:
   - Once set, lift the fudge out of the pan using the parchment paper or foil overhang. Cut into squares.

Enjoy your creamy and festive Peppermint Fudge!

Oatmeal Raisin Cookies

Ingredients:

- **For the Cookies:**
  - 1 cup (2 sticks) unsalted butter, softened

- 1 cup granulated sugar
- 1 cup packed brown sugar
- 2 large eggs
- 1 teaspoon vanilla extract
- 1 1/2 cups all-purpose flour
- 1 teaspoon baking soda
- 1/2 teaspoon baking powder
- 1/2 teaspoon salt
- 1 1/2 teaspoons ground cinnamon
- 3 cups old-fashioned rolled oats
- 1 cup raisins
- 1/2 cup chopped nuts (such as walnuts or pecans, optional)

Instructions:

1. **Preheat Oven**: Preheat your oven to 350°F (175°C). Line baking sheets with parchment paper or silicone baking mats.
2. **Cream Butter and Sugars**: In a large bowl, beat the softened butter, granulated sugar, and brown sugar together until light and fluffy.
3. **Add Eggs and Vanilla**: Beat in the eggs one at a time, then mix in the vanilla extract.
4. **Combine Dry Ingredients**: In another bowl, whisk together the flour, baking soda, baking powder, salt, and cinnamon.
5. **Mix Ingredients**: Gradually add the dry ingredients to the butter mixture, mixing until just combined. Stir in the oats, raisins, and nuts (if using).
6. **Drop Cookies**: Use a cookie scoop or tablespoon to drop rounded balls of dough onto the prepared baking sheets, spacing them about 2 inches apart.
7. **Bake**: Bake for 10-12 minutes, or until the edges are golden brown. The centers should be set but still soft.
8. **Cool**: Allow the cookies to cool on the baking sheets for a few minutes before transferring them to wire racks to cool completely.

Enjoy your delicious and hearty Oatmeal Raisin Cookies!

Walnut Caramel Bars

Ingredients:

- **For the Crust:**
  - 1 1/2 cups all-purpose flour

- 1/2 cup granulated sugar
- 1/2 cup (1 stick) unsalted butter, softened
- 1/4 teaspoon salt
- **For the Caramel Filling:**
    - 1/2 cup (1 stick) unsalted butter
    - 1 cup packed brown sugar
    - 1/4 cup light corn syrup
    - 1/4 cup heavy cream
    - 1/2 teaspoon vanilla extract
    - 1/2 teaspoon salt
- **For the Topping:**
    - 1 cup chopped walnuts
    - 1/4 cup granulated sugar (optional, for sprinkling on top)

Instructions:

1. **Preheat Oven**: Preheat your oven to 350°F (175°C). Grease or line an 8x8-inch baking pan with parchment paper.
2. **Prepare the Crust**:
    - In a medium bowl, combine the flour, granulated sugar, butter, and salt. Mix until the dough is crumbly and starts to come together.
    - Press the mixture evenly into the bottom of the prepared baking pan.
3. **Bake the Crust**:
    - Bake the crust in the preheated oven for 15 minutes, or until lightly golden.
4. **Prepare the Caramel Filling**:
    - In a medium saucepan, melt the butter over medium heat. Stir in the brown sugar, corn syrup, and heavy cream.
    - Bring the mixture to a boil, stirring constantly. Continue to cook for 2-3 minutes, or until the caramel thickens slightly and reaches 240°F (115°C) on a candy thermometer.
    - Remove from heat and stir in the vanilla extract and salt.
5. **Assemble the Bars**:
    - Pour the caramel filling over the baked crust, spreading it evenly with a spatula.
    - Sprinkle the chopped walnuts over the caramel. If desired, sprinkle with a little granulated sugar for extra crunch and sweetness.
6. **Bake Again**:
    - Return the pan to the oven and bake for an additional 15-20 minutes, or until the caramel is bubbly and the walnuts are lightly toasted.
7. **Cool and Slice**:
    - Allow the bars to cool completely in the pan before lifting them out using the parchment paper (if using).
    - Cut into squares or bars.

Enjoy these rich and chewy Walnut Caramel Bars with a cup of coffee or tea!

Lemon Bars

Ingredients:

- **For the Crust:**
    - 1 3/4 cups all-purpose flour

- 1/2 cup granulated sugar
- 1/4 teaspoon salt
- 1/2 cup (1 stick) unsalted butter, chilled and cut into pieces
- **For the Lemon Filling:**
    - 1 cup granulated sugar
    - 2 tablespoons all-purpose flour
    - 1/4 teaspoon baking powder
    - 4 large eggs
    - 1/2 cup freshly squeezed lemon juice (about 2-3 lemons)
    - Zest of 1 lemon
    - Powdered sugar, for dusting (optional)

Instructions:

1. **Preheat Oven**: Preheat your oven to 350°F (175°C). Line an 8x8-inch baking pan with parchment paper or lightly grease it.
2. **Prepare the Crust**:
    - In a medium bowl, combine the flour, granulated sugar, and salt.
    - Cut in the chilled butter using a pastry cutter or your fingers until the mixture resembles coarse crumbs.
    - Press the mixture evenly into the bottom of the prepared baking pan.
3. **Bake the Crust**:
    - Bake the crust in the preheated oven for 15-20 minutes, or until lightly golden. Remove from the oven and let cool slightly.
4. **Prepare the Lemon Filling**:
    - In a medium bowl, whisk together the granulated sugar, flour, and baking powder.
    - In another bowl, beat the eggs until light and frothy. Stir in the lemon juice and lemon zest.
    - Gradually add the sugar mixture to the egg mixture, whisking until well combined.
5. **Assemble and Bake**:
    - Pour the lemon filling over the partially baked crust.
    - Return the pan to the oven and bake for 20-25 minutes, or until the filling is set and the edges are lightly golden. The center should be just slightly jiggly.
6. **Cool and Slice**:
    - Allow the bars to cool completely in the pan on a wire rack.
    - Once cooled, lift the bars out of the pan using the parchment paper (if used) and cut into squares.
7. **Dust with Powdered Sugar** (optional):
    - Just before serving, dust the tops of the bars with powdered sugar for a nice finishing touch.

Enjoy your refreshing and tangy Lemon Bars!

Mocha Cookies

Ingredients:

- **For the Cookies:**
    - 1 cup (2 sticks) unsalted butter, softened
    - 1 cup granulated sugar

- 1 cup packed brown sugar
- 2 large eggs
- 2 teaspoons vanilla extract
- 2 1/4 cups all-purpose flour
- 1/2 cup unsweetened cocoa powder
- 1 teaspoon baking soda
- 1/2 teaspoon salt
- 2 tablespoons instant coffee granules or espresso powder
- 1 cup semi-sweet chocolate chips
- **For the Optional Drizzle:**
  - 1/2 cup semi-sweet chocolate chips
  - 2 tablespoons heavy cream

Instructions:

1. **Preheat Oven**: Preheat your oven to 350°F (175°C). Line baking sheets with parchment paper or silicone baking mats.
2. **Cream Butter and Sugars**: In a large bowl, beat the softened butter, granulated sugar, and brown sugar together until light and fluffy.
3. **Add Eggs and Vanilla**: Beat in the eggs one at a time, then mix in the vanilla extract.
4. **Prepare Dry Ingredients**:
   - In a separate bowl, whisk together the flour, cocoa powder, baking soda, and salt.
   - Dissolve the instant coffee granules in 1 tablespoon of hot water. Add this coffee mixture to the dry ingredients.
5. **Combine Ingredients**: Gradually add the dry ingredients to the butter mixture, mixing until just combined. Stir in the chocolate chips.
6. **Drop Cookies**: Use a cookie scoop or tablespoon to drop rounded balls of dough onto the prepared baking sheets, spacing them about 2 inches apart.
7. **Bake**: Bake for 10-12 minutes, or until the edges are set and the centers are still soft. Let cool on the baking sheets for a few minutes before transferring to wire racks to cool completely.
8. **Optional Drizzle**:
   - In a microwave-safe bowl, melt the chocolate chips and heavy cream together in 20-second intervals, stirring in between until smooth.
   - Drizzle the melted chocolate over the cooled cookies using a spoon or a piping bag.

Enjoy your delicious Mocha Cookies with a cup of coffee or as a special treat anytime!

Red Velvet Cake Balls

Ingredients:

- **For the Cake:**
    - 1 box (15.25 oz) red velvet cake mix
    - Ingredients required on the box (typically eggs, oil, and water)
- **For the Cream Cheese Frosting:**
    - 4 oz cream cheese, softened

- 1/4 cup unsalted butter, softened
- 1 cup powdered sugar
- 1/2 teaspoon vanilla extract
- **For Coating:**
    - 1 1/2 cups white chocolate chips or candy melts
    - 1 tablespoon vegetable oil or shortening (for melting)
- **For Decoration (optional):**
    - Sprinkles or crushed nuts

Instructions:

1. **Bake the Cake**:
    - Preheat your oven according to the cake mix package instructions.
    - Prepare the red velvet cake mix according to the package directions.
    - Bake in a 9x13-inch pan or according to package directions. Allow the cake to cool completely.
2. **Prepare the Cream Cheese Frosting**:
    - In a medium bowl, beat the softened cream cheese and butter together until creamy.
    - Gradually add the powdered sugar and beat until smooth and fluffy.
    - Mix in the vanilla extract.
3. **Crumble the Cake**:
    - Once the cake is completely cooled, crumble it into fine crumbs using your hands or a fork.
    - In a large bowl, mix the cake crumbs with the cream cheese frosting until well combined. The mixture should be moist enough to hold together when rolled into balls.
4. **Form Cake Balls**:
    - Use a cookie scoop or your hands to roll the mixture into 1-inch balls. Place them on a baking sheet lined with parchment paper.
    - Refrigerate the cake balls for at least 30 minutes to firm up.
5. **Prepare the Coating**:
    - In a microwave-safe bowl, melt the white chocolate chips and vegetable oil together in 20-second intervals, stirring in between, until smooth and fully melted.
6. **Dip the Cake Balls**:
    - Dip each chilled cake ball into the melted white chocolate, coating it completely. Use a fork or a toothpick to lift the ball out and tap off any excess chocolate.
    - Return the coated cake balls to the parchment-lined baking sheet.
7. **Decorate (optional)**:
    - While the coating is still wet, sprinkle with colored sprinkles or crushed nuts if desired.
8. **Chill and Set**:
    - Refrigerate the cake balls until the coating is set, about 30 minutes.

Enjoy your delightful Red Velvet Cake Balls as a sweet treat for any occasion!

Salted Caramel Brownies

Ingredients:

- **For the Brownies:**
    - 1/2 cup (1 stick) unsalted butter
    - 1 cup semi-sweet chocolate chips or chopped chocolate
    - 1 cup granulated sugar
    - 2 large eggs
    - 1 teaspoon vanilla extract
    - 1/2 cup all-purpose flour

- 1/4 teaspoon salt
- **For the Caramel Layer:**
    - 1/2 cup (1 stick) unsalted butter
    - 1 cup packed brown sugar
    - 1/4 cup light corn syrup
    - 1/4 cup heavy cream
    - 1/2 teaspoon vanilla extract
    - 1/4 teaspoon salt
- **For the Topping:**
    - Sea salt, for sprinkling

Instructions:

1. **Preheat Oven**: Preheat your oven to 350°F (175°C). Grease or line an 8x8-inch baking pan with parchment paper.
2. **Prepare the Brownies**:
    - In a medium saucepan, melt the butter and chocolate together over medium heat, stirring until smooth. Remove from heat.
    - Stir in the granulated sugar until well combined. Beat in the eggs one at a time, then mix in the vanilla extract.
    - Fold in the flour and salt until just combined.
    - Pour the brownie batter into the prepared baking pan and spread it evenly.
3. **Bake the Brownies**:
    - Bake the brownies for 20-25 minutes, or until a toothpick inserted into the center comes out with a few moist crumbs. The edges should be set.
    - Remove from the oven and let cool slightly while you prepare the caramel layer.
4. **Prepare the Caramel Layer**:
    - In a medium saucepan, melt the butter over medium heat.
    - Stir in the brown sugar and corn syrup, and bring to a boil, stirring constantly. Continue to boil for 2-3 minutes, or until the caramel thickens slightly.
    - Remove from heat and stir in the heavy cream, vanilla extract, and salt. Be cautious as the mixture may bubble up.
    - Allow the caramel to cool for a few minutes.
5. **Assemble the Brownies**:
    - Pour the warm caramel over the slightly cooled brownies, spreading it evenly with a spatula.
6. **Bake Again**:
    - Return the pan to the oven and bake for an additional 10 minutes, or until the caramel is bubbly.
7. **Cool and Add Topping**:
    - Remove the brownies from the oven and let them cool completely in the pan on a wire rack.
    - Once cooled, sprinkle with sea salt to taste.
8. **Slice and Serve**:
    - Once fully cooled, cut into squares and serve.

Enjoy your rich, decadent Salted Caramel Brownies with a delightful mix of chocolate, caramel, and a touch of sea salt!

Hazelnut Chocolate Truffles

Ingredients:

- **For the Truffles:**
    - 8 oz semi-sweet chocolate, finely chopped
    - 1/2 cup heavy cream
    - 2 tablespoons unsalted butter
    - 1/2 cup finely ground hazelnuts (from about 1/2 cup whole roasted hazelnuts)
    - 1 teaspoon vanilla extract
    - 1/4 teaspoon salt
- **For Coating:**

- 1/2 cup finely chopped hazelnuts
- 1/2 cup cocoa powder
- 1/2 cup melted chocolate (optional, for dipping)

Instructions:

1. **Prepare the Ganache**:
   - In a medium heatproof bowl, combine the finely chopped chocolate and unsalted butter.
   - In a small saucepan, heat the heavy cream over medium heat until it just begins to simmer.
   - Pour the hot cream over the chopped chocolate and butter. Let sit for 1-2 minutes to soften.
   - Stir the mixture until smooth and fully combined. Mix in the ground hazelnuts, vanilla extract, and salt.
2. **Chill the Ganache**:
   - Cover the bowl with plastic wrap and refrigerate for at least 2 hours, or until the ganache is firm enough to scoop.
3. **Form the Truffles**:
   - Once the ganache is chilled, use a small cookie scoop or a spoon to scoop out small balls of ganache. Roll them between your hands to form smooth, round truffles. Place them on a parchment-lined baking sheet.
4. **Coat the Truffles**:
   - Roll the truffles in finely chopped hazelnuts or cocoa powder to coat them. If using melted chocolate, dip each truffle into the melted chocolate, let the excess drip off, then roll in chopped hazelnuts or cocoa powder before the chocolate sets.
5. **Chill Again**:
   - Return the coated truffles to the refrigerator to set, about 30 minutes.
6. **Serve and Store**:
   - Enjoy your Hazelnut Chocolate Truffles! They can be stored in an airtight container in the refrigerator for up to 2 weeks.

These truffles are a luxurious treat with a delightful blend of rich chocolate and toasted hazelnuts. Enjoy!

Maple Pecan Cookies

Ingredients:

- **For the Cookies:**
    - 1 cup (2 sticks) unsalted butter, softened
    - 1 cup granulated sugar
    - 1/2 cup packed brown sugar
    - 1/2 cup pure maple syrup (not imitation maple syrup)
    - 1 large egg
    - 1 teaspoon vanilla extract
    - 2 1/4 cups all-purpose flour
    - 1 teaspoon baking soda

        - 1/2 teaspoon salt
        - 1 cup chopped pecans
- **For the Optional Maple Glaze:**
    - 1 cup powdered sugar
    - 2-3 tablespoons pure maple syrup
    - 1/2 teaspoon vanilla extract

Instructions:

1. **Preheat Oven**: Preheat your oven to 350°F (175°C). Line baking sheets with parchment paper or silicone baking mats.
2. **Cream Butter and Sugars**:
    - In a large bowl, beat the softened butter, granulated sugar, and brown sugar together until light and fluffy.
3. **Add Wet Ingredients**:
    - Mix in the maple syrup, egg, and vanilla extract until well combined.
4. **Combine Dry Ingredients**:
    - In another bowl, whisk together the flour, baking soda, and salt.
5. **Mix Dough**:
    - Gradually add the dry ingredients to the butter mixture, mixing until just combined. Fold in the chopped pecans.
6. **Drop Cookies**:
    - Use a cookie scoop or tablespoon to drop rounded balls of dough onto the prepared baking sheets, spacing them about 2 inches apart.
7. **Bake**:
    - Bake for 10-12 minutes, or until the edges are lightly golden. The centers should be soft but set.
8. **Cool**:
    - Allow the cookies to cool on the baking sheets for a few minutes before transferring them to wire racks to cool completely.
9. **Optional Maple Glaze**:
    - In a small bowl, whisk together the powdered sugar, maple syrup, and vanilla extract until smooth. Adjust the consistency with more maple syrup if needed.
    - Drizzle the glaze over the cooled cookies using a spoon or a piping bag.

Enjoy your Maple Pecan Cookies with their delicious maple flavor and crunchy pecans!

Butterscotch Blondies

Ingredients:

- **For the Blondies:**
    - 1 cup (2 sticks) unsalted butter, softened
    - 1 cup packed brown sugar
    - 1/2 cup granulated sugar
    - 2 large eggs
    - 2 teaspoons vanilla extract
    - 2 cups all-purpose flour
    - 1 teaspoon baking powder
    - 1/2 teaspoon salt
    - 1 cup butterscotch chips (or chunks)

- **For Optional Topping:**
  - 1/4 cup butterscotch chips (for sprinkling on top)

Instructions:

1. **Preheat Oven**: Preheat your oven to 350°F (175°C). Grease or line a 9x13-inch baking pan with parchment paper.
2. **Cream Butter and Sugars**:
   - In a large bowl, beat the softened butter, brown sugar, and granulated sugar together until light and fluffy.
3. **Add Eggs and Vanilla**:
   - Beat in the eggs one at a time, then mix in the vanilla extract until fully combined.
4. **Combine Dry Ingredients**:
   - In a separate bowl, whisk together the flour, baking powder, and salt.
5. **Mix Dough**:
   - Gradually add the dry ingredients to the butter mixture, mixing until just combined. Stir in the butterscotch chips.
6. **Spread and Bake**:
   - Spread the batter evenly into the prepared baking pan. If desired, sprinkle the additional 1/4 cup of butterscotch chips on top.
7. **Bake**:
   - Bake for 25-30 minutes, or until a toothpick inserted into the center comes out clean and the edges are golden brown.
8. **Cool and Slice**:
   - Allow the blondies to cool completely in the pan on a wire rack. Once cooled, cut into squares or bars.

These Butterscotch Blondies are chewy and sweet with a delightful butterscotch flavor. Enjoy them as a snack or a dessert!

Nutmeg Spice Cake

Ingredients:

- **For the Cake:**
  - 1 1/2 cups all-purpose flour
  - 1 cup granulated sugar
  - 1/2 cup packed brown sugar
  - 1/2 teaspoon baking powder
  - 1/2 teaspoon baking soda
  - 1/2 teaspoon salt
  - 1 1/2 teaspoons ground nutmeg
  - 1 teaspoon ground cinnamon
  - 1/2 teaspoon ground cloves

- 1/2 teaspoon ground ginger
- 1/2 cup (1 stick) unsalted butter, softened
- 2 large eggs
- 1/2 cup milk
- 1/2 cup sour cream
- 1/4 cup molasses
- 1 teaspoon vanilla extract
- **For the Optional Glaze:**
    - 1 cup powdered sugar
    - 2-3 tablespoons milk
    - 1/4 teaspoon vanilla extract

Instructions:

1. **Preheat Oven**: Preheat your oven to 350°F (175°C). Grease and flour an 8-inch round cake pan or line it with parchment paper.
2. **Combine Dry Ingredients**:
    - In a medium bowl, whisk together the flour, granulated sugar, brown sugar, baking powder, baking soda, salt, nutmeg, cinnamon, cloves, and ginger.
3. **Cream Butter and Sugar**:
    - In a large bowl, beat the softened butter until creamy. Gradually add the granulated sugar and brown sugar, beating until light and fluffy.
4. **Add Eggs and Wet Ingredients**:
    - Beat in the eggs one at a time, mixing well after each addition. Mix in the milk, sour cream, molasses, and vanilla extract until well combined.
5. **Mix Dry and Wet Ingredients**:
    - Gradually add the dry ingredients to the wet ingredients, mixing until just combined. Be careful not to overmix.
6. **Bake**:
    - Pour the batter into the prepared cake pan and smooth the top.
    - Bake for 25-30 minutes, or until a toothpick inserted into the center comes out clean and the cake springs back when lightly touched.
7. **Cool**:
    - Allow the cake to cool in the pan for 10 minutes before transferring it to a wire rack to cool completely.
8. **Optional Glaze**:
    - In a small bowl, whisk together the powdered sugar, milk, and vanilla extract until smooth. Adjust the consistency with more milk if necessary.
    - Drizzle the glaze over the cooled cake.

Enjoy your Nutmeg Spice Cake with a cup of tea or coffee for a comforting treat!

Cinnamon Roll Cookies

Ingredients:

- **For the Cookies:**
    - 1 cup (2 sticks) unsalted butter, softened
    - 1 cup granulated sugar
    - 1/2 cup packed brown sugar
    - 2 large eggs
    - 1 teaspoon vanilla extract
    - 2 1/2 cups all-purpose flour
    - 1/2 teaspoon baking powder
    - 1/4 teaspoon baking soda
    - 1/4 teaspoon salt
- **For the Cinnamon Sugar Filling:**

- 1/2 cup granulated sugar
- 2 tablespoons ground cinnamon
- **For the Glaze:**
  - 1 cup powdered sugar
  - 2-3 tablespoons milk
  - 1/2 teaspoon vanilla extract

Instructions:

1. **Preheat Oven**: Preheat your oven to 350°F (175°C). Line baking sheets with parchment paper or silicone baking mats.
2. **Prepare the Dough**:
   - In a large bowl, cream the softened butter, granulated sugar, and brown sugar together until light and fluffy.
   - Beat in the eggs one at a time, then mix in the vanilla extract.
3. **Combine Dry Ingredients**:
   - In a separate bowl, whisk together the flour, baking powder, baking soda, and salt.
   - Gradually add the dry ingredients to the butter mixture, mixing until just combined.
4. **Roll and Fill**:
   - On a lightly floured surface, roll out the dough into a rectangle about 1/4 inch thick.
   - In a small bowl, combine the granulated sugar and ground cinnamon for the filling. Sprinkle the cinnamon sugar mixture evenly over the rolled-out dough.
5. **Shape Cookies**:
   - Starting from one edge, carefully roll up the dough into a log, pinching the seam to seal.
   - Slice the dough log into 1/2-inch thick slices and place them on the prepared baking sheets.
6. **Bake**:
   - Bake for 10-12 minutes, or until the edges are lightly golden. The centers should be soft but set.
7. **Cool**:
   - Allow the cookies to cool on the baking sheets for a few minutes before transferring them to wire racks to cool completely.
8. **Prepare the Glaze**:
   - In a small bowl, whisk together the powdered sugar, milk, and vanilla extract until smooth. Adjust the consistency with more milk if necessary.
9. **Glaze Cookies**:
   - Drizzle the glaze over the cooled cookies using a spoon or a piping bag.

Enjoy these delightful Cinnamon Roll Cookies with their sweet cinnamon filling and creamy glaze!

Raspberry Almond Thumbprints

Ingredients:

- **For the Cookies:**
    - 1 cup (2 sticks) unsalted butter, softened
    - 1/2 cup granulated sugar
    - 1/2 cup packed brown sugar
    - 1 large egg yolk
    - 1 teaspoon almond extract
    - 2 cups all-purpose flour
    - 1/2 cup finely ground almonds (or almond meal)
    - 1/4 teaspoon salt
- **For the Filling:**
    - 1/2 cup raspberry jam or preserves

- Optional: fresh raspberries for garnish
- **For the Optional Glaze:**
    - 1/2 cup powdered sugar
    - 1-2 tablespoons milk
    - 1/4 teaspoon almond extract

Instructions:

1. **Preheat Oven**: Preheat your oven to 350°F (175°C). Line baking sheets with parchment paper or silicone baking mats.
2. **Prepare the Dough**:
    - In a large bowl, cream the softened butter, granulated sugar, and brown sugar together until light and fluffy.
    - Beat in the egg yolk and almond extract until well combined.
3. **Combine Dry Ingredients**:
    - In a separate bowl, whisk together the flour, finely ground almonds, and salt.
    - Gradually add the dry ingredients to the butter mixture, mixing until just combined.
4. **Shape Cookies**:
    - Scoop tablespoon-sized portions of dough and roll them into balls. Place the balls on the prepared baking sheets, spacing them about 2 inches apart.
    - Using your thumb or the back of a spoon, make an indentation in the center of each dough ball.
5. **Fill with Jam**:
    - Spoon a small amount of raspberry jam into each indentation.
6. **Bake**:
    - Bake for 12-15 minutes, or until the edges of the cookies are lightly golden. The jam should be bubbly.
7. **Cool**:
    - Allow the cookies to cool on the baking sheets for a few minutes before transferring them to wire racks to cool completely.
8. **Optional Glaze**:
    - In a small bowl, whisk together the powdered sugar, milk, and almond extract until smooth. Adjust the consistency with more milk if necessary.
    - Drizzle the glaze over the cooled cookies if desired.
9. **Garnish (optional)**:
    - Garnish with fresh raspberries if you like.

Enjoy these delightful Raspberry Almond Thumbprints with their buttery almond base and sweet raspberry center!

Gingerbread Whoopie Pies

Ingredients:

- **For the Gingerbread Cookies:**
    - 2 1/4 cups all-purpose flour
    - 1/2 teaspoon baking soda
    - 1/2 teaspoon baking powder
    - 1/2 teaspoon salt
    - 1 tablespoon ground ginger
    - 1 tablespoon ground cinnamon
    - 1/2 teaspoon ground cloves
    - 1/2 teaspoon ground nutmeg
    - 1/2 cup (1 stick) unsalted butter, softened
    - 1/2 cup granulated sugar
    - 1/2 cup packed brown sugar

- 1 large egg
- 1/2 cup molasses
- **For the Cream Cheese Filling:**
    - 1/2 cup (1 stick) unsalted butter, softened
    - 4 oz cream cheese, softened
    - 2 cups powdered sugar
    - 1 teaspoon vanilla extract

Instructions:

1. **Preheat Oven**: Preheat your oven to 350°F (175°C). Line baking sheets with parchment paper or silicone baking mats.
2. **Prepare the Gingerbread Cookies**:
    - In a medium bowl, whisk together the flour, baking soda, baking powder, salt, ginger, cinnamon, cloves, and nutmeg.
    - In a large bowl, cream the softened butter, granulated sugar, and brown sugar together until light and fluffy.
    - Beat in the egg, then mix in the molasses until fully combined.
    - Gradually add the dry ingredients to the wet ingredients, mixing until just combined.
3. **Scoop and Bake**:
    - Use a cookie scoop or tablespoon to drop rounded balls of dough onto the prepared baking sheets, spacing them about 2 inches apart.
    - Flatten each dough ball slightly with the back of a spoon or your fingers.
    - Bake for 10-12 minutes, or until the edges are set and the centers are just starting to firm up. Allow to cool on the baking sheets for a few minutes before transferring to wire racks to cool completely.
4. **Prepare the Cream Cheese Filling**:
    - In a medium bowl, beat the softened butter and cream cheese together until creamy.
    - Gradually add the powdered sugar, beating until smooth and fluffy.
    - Mix in the vanilla extract.
5. **Assemble the Whoopie Pies**:
    - Once the cookies are completely cooled, spread or pipe a generous amount of cream cheese filling onto the flat side of one cookie.
    - Top with another cookie, flat side down, to create a sandwich.
6. **Serve and Store**:
    - Enjoy your Gingerbread Whoopie Pies immediately, or store them in an airtight container in the refrigerator for up to 1 week.

These Gingerbread Whoopie Pies are perfect for the holidays or any time you crave a spiced treat with a creamy twist!

Poppy Seed Bread

Ingredients:

- **For the Bread:**
    - 2 cups all-purpose flour
    - 1 1/2 teaspoons baking powder
    - 1/4 teaspoon salt
    - 1/2 cup (1 stick) unsalted butter, softened
    - 1 cup granulated sugar
    - 2 large eggs
    - 1 cup milk
    - 2 tablespoons poppy seeds
    - 1 tablespoon lemon zest (optional, for added flavor)
    - 1 teaspoon vanilla extract
- **For the Glaze (optional):**
    - 1/2 cup powdered sugar

- 2 tablespoons lemon juice (or milk)
- 1/2 teaspoon vanilla extract

Instructions:

1. **Preheat Oven**: Preheat your oven to 350°F (175°C). Grease and flour a 9x5-inch loaf pan or line it with parchment paper.
2. **Prepare Dry Ingredients**:
    - In a medium bowl, whisk together the flour, baking powder, and salt. Set aside.
3. **Cream Butter and Sugar**:
    - In a large bowl, beat the softened butter and granulated sugar together until light and fluffy.
4. **Add Eggs and Flavorings**:
    - Beat in the eggs one at a time, mixing well after each addition.
    - Mix in the vanilla extract and lemon zest (if using).
5. **Combine Wet and Dry Ingredients**:
    - Gradually add the dry ingredients to the butter mixture, alternating with the milk. Begin and end with the dry ingredients, mixing just until combined.
    - Stir in the poppy seeds.
6. **Bake**:
    - Pour the batter into the prepared loaf pan and smooth the top.
    - Bake for 50-60 minutes, or until a toothpick inserted into the center of the bread comes out clean. The bread should be golden brown and spring back when lightly touched.
7. **Cool**:
    - Allow the bread to cool in the pan for about 10 minutes before transferring it to a wire rack to cool completely.
8. **Optional Glaze**:
    - While the bread is cooling, prepare the glaze by whisking together the powdered sugar, lemon juice (or milk), and vanilla extract until smooth.
    - Drizzle the glaze over the cooled bread.

This Poppy Seed Bread is perfect for breakfast, a snack, or even as a light dessert. Enjoy its moist texture and delightful poppy seed crunch!

Peppermint Hot Chocolate Cookies

Ingredients:

- **For the Cookies:**
    - 1 cup (2 sticks) unsalted butter, softened
    - 1 cup granulated sugar
    - 1/2 cup packed brown sugar
    - 2 large eggs
    - 1 teaspoon vanilla extract
    - 2 1/4 cups all-purpose flour
    - 1/2 cup unsweetened cocoa powder
    - 1/2 teaspoon baking soda
    - 1/2 teaspoon baking powder
    - 1/4 teaspoon salt
    - 1 cup mini marshmallows
    - 1/2 cup crushed peppermint candies or candy canes

- **For the Optional Frosting:**
    - 1 cup powdered sugar
    - 2 tablespoons unsweetened cocoa powder
    - 2-3 tablespoons milk
    - 1/2 teaspoon vanilla extract
    - 1/4 teaspoon peppermint extract
- **For Garnish (optional):**
    - Additional crushed peppermint candies or candy canes

Instructions:

1. **Preheat Oven**: Preheat your oven to 350°F (175°C). Line baking sheets with parchment paper or silicone baking mats.
2. **Prepare the Cookie Dough**:
    - In a large bowl, cream the softened butter, granulated sugar, and brown sugar together until light and fluffy.
    - Beat in the eggs one at a time, mixing well after each addition. Mix in the vanilla extract.
3. **Combine Dry Ingredients**:
    - In a separate bowl, whisk together the flour, cocoa powder, baking soda, baking powder, and salt.
4. **Mix Dry and Wet Ingredients**:
    - Gradually add the dry ingredients to the butter mixture, mixing until just combined.
    - Fold in the mini marshmallows and crushed peppermint candies.
5. **Shape and Bake**:
    - Drop rounded tablespoonfuls of dough onto the prepared baking sheets, spacing them about 2 inches apart.
    - Bake for 10-12 minutes, or until the cookies are set but still soft in the center.
6. **Cool**:
    - Allow the cookies to cool on the baking sheets for a few minutes before transferring them to wire racks to cool completely.
7. **Optional Frosting**:
    - While the cookies are cooling, prepare the frosting by whisking together the powdered sugar, cocoa powder, milk, vanilla extract, and peppermint extract until smooth. Adjust the consistency with more milk if needed.
    - Spread or pipe the frosting onto the cooled cookies.
8. **Garnish**:
    - If using, sprinkle additional crushed peppermint candies or candy canes on top of the frosting before it sets.

Enjoy your Peppermint Hot Chocolate Cookies with their rich chocolate flavor, sweet marshmallow bits, and festive peppermint crunch!

Chewy Molasses Cookies

Ingredients:

- **For the Cookies:**
    - 1 cup (2 sticks) unsalted butter, softened
    - 1 cup granulated sugar, plus more for rolling
    - 1/2 cup packed brown sugar
    - 1/2 cup molasses
    - 1 large egg
    - 2 1/4 cups all-purpose flour
    - 2 teaspoons ground ginger
    - 1 1/2 teaspoons ground cinnamon
    - 1/2 teaspoon ground cloves
    - 1/2 teaspoon baking soda
    - 1/4 teaspoon salt
- **For Rolling (optional):**

- Granulated sugar for rolling

Instructions:

1. **Preheat Oven**: Preheat your oven to 350°F (175°C). Line baking sheets with parchment paper or silicone baking mats.
2. **Cream Butter and Sugars**:
    - In a large bowl, beat the softened butter, granulated sugar, and brown sugar together until light and fluffy.
3. **Add Molasses and Egg**:
    - Mix in the molasses and egg until fully combined.
4. **Combine Dry Ingredients**:
    - In a separate bowl, whisk together the flour, ginger, cinnamon, cloves, baking soda, and salt.
5. **Mix Dry and Wet Ingredients**:
    - Gradually add the dry ingredients to the butter mixture, mixing until just combined.
6. **Shape Cookies**:
    - Scoop tablespoon-sized portions of dough and roll them into balls. Roll each ball in granulated sugar if desired.
    - Place the dough balls on the prepared baking sheets, spacing them about 2 inches apart. Flatten each ball slightly with the bottom of a glass or your fingers.
7. **Bake**:
    - Bake for 10-12 minutes, or until the edges are set and the centers are slightly soft. The cookies will continue to set as they cool.
8. **Cool**:
    - Allow the cookies to cool on the baking sheets for a few minutes before transferring them to wire racks to cool completely.

Enjoy your Chewy Molasses Cookies with their rich, spiced flavor and delightful chewy texture! They're perfect with a cup of tea or coffee.

Cranberry Almond Granola Bars

Ingredients:

- **For the Granola Bars:**
    - 2 cups old-fashioned rolled oats
    - 1 cup slivered almonds
    - 1 cup dried cranberries
    - 1/2 cup honey or maple syrup
    - 1/2 cup natural almond butter (or peanut butter)
    - 1/4 cup brown sugar (packed)
    - 1/2 teaspoon vanilla extract
    - 1/4 teaspoon salt
    - Optional: 1/4 cup mini chocolate chips or white chocolate chips

Instructions:

1. **Preheat Oven**: Preheat your oven to 350°F (175°C). Line an 8x8-inch baking pan with parchment paper, leaving an overhang on the sides for easy removal.
2. **Toast Oats and Almonds**:
    - Spread the rolled oats and slivered almonds on a baking sheet. Toast in the oven for about 8-10 minutes, stirring halfway through, until golden and fragrant. Remove from oven and let cool.
3. **Prepare the Sticky Mixture**:
    - In a medium saucepan, combine the honey (or maple syrup), almond butter, and brown sugar. Cook over medium heat, stirring constantly, until the mixture is smooth and the sugar has dissolved, about 2-3 minutes.
    - Remove from heat and stir in the vanilla extract and salt.
4. **Combine Ingredients**:
    - In a large bowl, combine the toasted oats, slivered almonds, dried cranberries, and mini chocolate chips (if using).
    - Pour the sticky mixture over the dry ingredients and stir until everything is well coated and combined.
5. **Press into Pan**:
    - Transfer the mixture to the prepared baking pan. Press it down firmly and evenly using the back of a spoon or your hands to ensure the bars will hold together.
6. **Cool and Set**:
    - Allow the mixture to cool completely in the pan, about 2 hours. For quicker cooling, you can place the pan in the refrigerator.
7. **Cut into Bars**:
    - Once cooled and set, lift the granola mixture out of the pan using the parchment paper overhang. Transfer to a cutting board and cut into bars or squares.
8. **Store**:
    - Store the granola bars in an airtight container at room temperature for up to a week. For longer storage, keep them in the refrigerator.

These Cranberry Almond Granola Bars are chewy, crunchy, and packed with flavor, making them a great option for a nutritious snack or on-the-go breakfast!

Chocolate Chip Pretzel Cookies

Ingredients:

- **For the Cookies:**
    - 1 cup (2 sticks) unsalted butter, softened
    - 1 cup granulated sugar
    - 1 cup packed brown sugar
    - 2 large eggs
    - 1 teaspoon vanilla extract
    - 2 1/4 cups all-purpose flour
    - 1/2 teaspoon baking powder
    - 1/2 teaspoon baking soda
    - 1/4 teaspoon salt
    - 1 cup chocolate chips (semi-sweet or milk chocolate)
    - 1 cup pretzel pieces (crushed or broken into small chunks)
- **For Optional Topping:**

- Coarse sea salt or pretzel pieces for sprinkling on top

Instructions:

1. **Preheat Oven**: Preheat your oven to 350°F (175°C). Line baking sheets with parchment paper or silicone baking mats.
2. **Cream Butter and Sugars**:
    - In a large bowl, beat the softened butter, granulated sugar, and brown sugar together until light and fluffy.
3. **Add Eggs and Vanilla**:
    - Beat in the eggs one at a time, mixing well after each addition. Mix in the vanilla extract.
4. **Combine Dry Ingredients**:
    - In a separate bowl, whisk together the flour, baking powder, baking soda, and salt.
5. **Mix Dry and Wet Ingredients**:
    - Gradually add the dry ingredients to the butter mixture, mixing until just combined.
6. **Add Chocolate Chips and Pretzels**:
    - Fold in the chocolate chips and pretzel pieces until evenly distributed throughout the dough.
7. **Shape and Bake**:
    - Drop rounded tablespoonfuls of dough onto the prepared baking sheets, spacing them about 2 inches apart.
    - If desired, sprinkle a few additional pretzel pieces or a pinch of coarse sea salt on top of each cookie before baking.
8. **Bake**:
    - Bake for 10-12 minutes, or until the edges are lightly golden and the centers are set. The cookies will continue to firm up as they cool.
9. **Cool**:
    - Allow the cookies to cool on the baking sheets for a few minutes before transferring them to wire racks to cool completely.

These Chocolate Chip Pretzel Cookies offer a delightful combination of sweet and salty flavors, with a satisfying crunch from the pretzels and richness from the chocolate chips!

Bourbon Balls

Ingredients:

- **For the Bourbon Balls:**
    - 1 cup crushed vanilla wafers (about 30-35 wafers)
    - 1 cup finely chopped nuts (walnuts, pecans, or almonds)
    - 1 cup powdered sugar
    - 2 tablespoons unsweetened cocoa powder
    - 1/4 cup corn syrup (light or dark)
    - 1/4 cup bourbon
    - 1/2 teaspoon vanilla extract
- **For Rolling (optional):**
    - Additional powdered sugar
    - Additional crushed nuts
    - Additional cocoa powder

Instructions:

1. **Prepare Ingredients**:
   - In a large bowl, combine the crushed vanilla wafers, finely chopped nuts, powdered sugar, and cocoa powder.
2. **Add Wet Ingredients**:
   - In a separate bowl, mix together the corn syrup, bourbon, and vanilla extract.
3. **Combine Mixtures**:
   - Pour the wet ingredients into the dry ingredients and mix until everything is well combined and holds together when pressed.
4. **Shape the Balls**:
   - Using your hands or a small cookie scoop, form the mixture into 1-inch balls. Place them on a baking sheet or plate lined with parchment paper.
5. **Roll in Coating (optional)**:
   - If desired, roll the bourbon balls in additional powdered sugar, crushed nuts, or cocoa powder to coat them.
6. **Chill**:
   - Refrigerate the bourbon balls for at least 2 hours or until firm. They can also be stored in an airtight container in the refrigerator for up to 2 weeks.
7. **Serve**:
   - Serve chilled or at room temperature.

Enjoy these Bourbon Balls as a delightful, boozy treat that's perfect for the holiday season or any special occasion!

Sweet Potato Pie Bars

Ingredients:

- **For the Crust:**
    - 1 1/2 cups graham cracker crumbs
    - 1/4 cup granulated sugar
    - 1/2 cup (1 stick) unsalted butter, melted
- **For the Filling:**
    - 2 cups mashed sweet potatoes (about 2 medium sweet potatoes)
    - 1 cup granulated sugar
    - 1/2 cup packed brown sugar
    - 1/2 cup evaporated milk
    - 1/4 cup milk
    - 2 large eggs
    - 1 teaspoon vanilla extract
    - 1 teaspoon ground cinnamon
    - 1/2 teaspoon ground nutmeg
    - 1/4 teaspoon ground ginger

- ○ 1/4 teaspoon salt
- **For the Optional Topping:**
  - ○ Whipped cream or marshmallows for serving

Instructions:

1. **Preheat Oven**: Preheat your oven to 350°F (175°C). Grease or line an 8x8-inch baking pan with parchment paper, leaving an overhang for easy removal.
2. **Prepare the Crust**:
   - ○ In a medium bowl, combine the graham cracker crumbs, granulated sugar, and melted butter. Mix until the crumbs are evenly coated and the mixture resembles wet sand.
   - ○ Press the crumb mixture evenly into the bottom of the prepared baking pan to form the crust.
3. **Bake the Crust**:
   - ○ Bake the crust for 8-10 minutes, or until set and slightly golden. Remove from the oven and let it cool while you prepare the filling.
4. **Prepare the Filling**:
   - ○ In a large bowl, combine the mashed sweet potatoes, granulated sugar, brown sugar, evaporated milk, milk, eggs, vanilla extract, cinnamon, nutmeg, ginger, and salt. Mix until smooth and well combined.
5. **Pour and Bake**:
   - ○ Pour the sweet potato filling over the cooled crust, spreading it evenly with a spatula.
   - ○ Bake for 40-45 minutes, or until the filling is set and the edges are slightly firm. The center should be just slightly jiggly.
6. **Cool**:
   - ○ Allow the bars to cool completely in the pan on a wire rack. For best results, chill in the refrigerator for at least 2 hours to make cutting easier.
7. **Cut and Serve**:
   - ○ Once chilled and set, lift the bars out of the pan using the parchment paper overhang. Cut into squares.
   - ○ Serve with a dollop of whipped cream or a few marshmallows if desired.

These Sweet Potato Pie Bars offer a delicious, portable version of the classic pie, perfect for gatherings or a special treat!

Chocolate Dipped Pretzels

Ingredients:

- **For the Pretzels:**
    - 1 cup semi-sweet or milk chocolate chips
    - 1 cup white chocolate chips (optional for drizzling)
    - 12-16 pretzel rods or pretzel twists (about 1 cup)
    - 1/2 cup crushed candy canes, sprinkles, or chopped nuts (optional for decoration)

Instructions:

1. **Prepare Work Area:**
    - Line a baking sheet with parchment paper or a silicone baking mat. This will help the chocolate-dipped pretzels not stick and make cleanup easier.
2. **Melt the Chocolate:**
    - In separate microwave-safe bowls, melt the semi-sweet (or milk) chocolate chips and white chocolate chips. Heat in 30-second intervals, stirring between each,

until smooth and fully melted. Alternatively, you can use a double boiler to melt the chocolate over simmering water.
3. **Dip the Pretzels**:
    - Dip each pretzel into the melted chocolate, covering about half to three-quarters of the pretzel. Gently shake off any excess chocolate.
4. **Add Decorations (Optional)**:
    - If desired, immediately sprinkle the dipped pretzels with crushed candy canes, sprinkles, or chopped nuts before the chocolate sets. This adds both color and texture.
5. **Drizzle with White Chocolate (Optional)**:
    - If you're using white chocolate for drizzling, transfer it to a small plastic bag or piping bag with a small hole cut in the tip. Drizzle the white chocolate over the dipped pretzels in a zigzag pattern for a decorative touch.
6. **Cool and Set**:
    - Place the dipped pretzels on the prepared baking sheet. Allow the chocolate to set at room temperature, or speed up the process by placing them in the refrigerator for about 10-15 minutes.
7. **Store**:
    - Once the chocolate is set, store the pretzels in an airtight container at room temperature for up to 1 week. They can also be refrigerated if you prefer them extra crispy.

These Chocolate-Dipped Pretzels are a crowd-pleaser and make a fantastic gift when packaged in a decorative box or tin. Enjoy the crunchy, salty-sweet combination!

Carrot Cake Cupcakes

Ingredients:

- **For the Cupcakes:**
    - 1 1/2 cups all-purpose flour
    - 1 teaspoon baking powder
    - 1/2 teaspoon baking soda
    - 1/2 teaspoon salt
    - 1 teaspoon ground cinnamon
    - 1/2 teaspoon ground nutmeg
    - 1/4 teaspoon ground cloves
    - 1/2 cup vegetable oil
    - 1/2 cup granulated sugar
    - 1/2 cup packed brown sugar
    - 2 large eggs
    - 1 cup finely grated carrots (about 2 medium carrots)
    - 1/2 cup crushed pineapple, drained
    - 1/2 cup chopped walnuts or pecans (optional)

- 1/4 cup shredded coconut (optional)
- **For the Cream Cheese Frosting:**
    - 8 oz (1 package) cream cheese, softened
    - 1/2 cup (1 stick) unsalted butter, softened
    - 4 cups powdered sugar
    - 1 teaspoon vanilla extract

Instructions:

1. **Preheat Oven**: Preheat your oven to 350°F (175°C). Line a 12-cup muffin tin with cupcake liners.
2. **Prepare Dry Ingredients**:
    - In a medium bowl, whisk together the flour, baking powder, baking soda, salt, cinnamon, nutmeg, and cloves. Set aside.
3. **Mix Wet Ingredients**:
    - In a large bowl, whisk together the oil, granulated sugar, and brown sugar until well combined.
    - Beat in the eggs one at a time, mixing well after each addition.
4. **Combine Ingredients**:
    - Gradually add the dry ingredients to the wet ingredients, mixing just until combined.
    - Fold in the grated carrots, crushed pineapple, walnuts or pecans (if using), and shredded coconut (if using).
5. **Fill Cupcake Liners**:
    - Divide the batter evenly among the 12 cupcake liners, filling each about 2/3 full.
6. **Bake**:
    - Bake for 18-22 minutes, or until a toothpick inserted into the center of a cupcake comes out clean.
7. **Cool**:
    - Allow the cupcakes to cool in the tin for about 5 minutes before transferring them to a wire rack to cool completely.
8. **Prepare Cream Cheese Frosting**:
    - In a large bowl, beat the softened cream cheese and butter together until creamy and smooth.
    - Gradually add the powdered sugar, beating until well combined and smooth.
    - Mix in the vanilla extract.
9. **Frost the Cupcakes**:
    - Once the cupcakes are completely cooled, frost them with the cream cheese frosting using a piping bag or a spatula.
10. **Serve and Store**:
    - Serve immediately or store the frosted cupcakes in the refrigerator for up to 3 days. They can also be frozen for up to 2 months if un-frosted.

Enjoy these Carrot Cake Cupcakes with their moist texture and delicious cream cheese frosting! They make a wonderful treat for any occasion.

Almond Joy Bars

Ingredients:

- **For the Coconut Layer:**
    - 2 1/2 cups sweetened shredded coconut
    - 1 cup sweetened condensed milk
    - 1/4 cup unsalted butter, melted
    - 1 teaspoon vanilla extract
- **For the Almond Layer:**
    - 24 whole almonds (or as many as needed for topping)
- **For the Chocolate Layer:**
    - 1 1/2 cups semi-sweet or milk chocolate chips
    - 1 tablespoon coconut oil (optional, for smooth melting)

Instructions:

1. **Preheat Oven**: Preheat your oven to 350°F (175°C). Line an 8x8-inch baking pan with parchment paper or aluminum foil, leaving an overhang for easy removal.
2. **Prepare the Coconut Layer**:

- In a large bowl, mix together the shredded coconut, sweetened condensed milk, melted butter, and vanilla extract until well combined.
- Press the mixture evenly into the bottom of the prepared baking pan, creating an even layer.

3. **Bake the Coconut Layer**:
   - Bake for 10-12 minutes, or until the edges are golden brown. Remove from the oven and let cool slightly.
4. **Add the Almonds**:
   - Place the almonds evenly on top of the slightly cooled coconut layer, pressing them in gently.
5. **Prepare the Chocolate Layer**:
   - In a microwave-safe bowl, melt the chocolate chips with the coconut oil (if using) in 30-second intervals, stirring in between, until smooth and fully melted. You can also melt the chocolate using a double boiler.
6. **Top with Chocolate**:
   - Pour the melted chocolate over the almond layer, spreading it evenly with a spatula.
7. **Cool and Set**:
   - Refrigerate the bars for at least 2 hours, or until the chocolate is set and the bars are firm.
8. **Cut and Serve**:
   - Once the bars are fully set, lift them out of the pan using the parchment paper or foil overhang. Cut into squares or rectangles.
9. **Store**:
   - Store the Almond Joy Bars in an airtight container at room temperature for up to 1 week. For longer storage, keep them in the refrigerator.

These Almond Joy Bars offer a delightful combination of flavors and textures, making them a perfect treat for any occasion!

Sticky Toffee Pudding Cake

Ingredients:

- **For the Cake:**
    - 1 cup (200g) pitted dates, chopped
    - 1 cup (240ml) boiling water
    - 1 teaspoon baking soda
    - 1/2 cup (1 stick) unsalted butter, softened
    - 1/2 cup granulated sugar
    - 1/2 cup packed brown sugar
    - 2 large eggs
    - 1 cup all-purpose flour
    - 1 teaspoon baking powder
    - 1/2 teaspoon salt
    - 1 teaspoon vanilla extract
- **For the Toffee Sauce:**
    - 1 cup (200g) packed brown sugar
    - 1/2 cup (1 stick) unsalted butter
    - 1/2 cup heavy cream
    - 1 teaspoon vanilla extract

Instructions:

1. **Preheat Oven**: Preheat your oven to 350°F (175°C). Grease and flour an 8-inch square baking dish or a similar-sized cake pan.
2. **Prepare the Dates**:
    - In a medium bowl, combine the chopped dates and boiling water. Stir in the baking soda and let it sit for about 10 minutes to soften the dates.
3. **Mix Cake Batter**:
    - In a large bowl, cream together the softened butter, granulated sugar, and brown sugar until light and fluffy.
    - Beat in the eggs one at a time, mixing well after each addition. Stir in the vanilla extract.
    - In another bowl, whisk together the flour, baking powder, and salt.
    - Gradually add the dry ingredients to the wet ingredients, mixing until just combined.
4. **Combine Dates and Batter**:
    - Gently fold the date mixture (including any liquid) into the cake batter until evenly combined.
5. **Bake**:
    - Pour the batter into the prepared baking dish, spreading it evenly.
    - Bake for 30-35 minutes, or until a toothpick inserted into the center comes out clean and the top is set.
6. **Prepare the Toffee Sauce**:
    - While the cake is baking, make the toffee sauce. In a medium saucepan, combine the brown sugar, butter, and heavy cream.
    - Cook over medium heat, stirring constantly until the mixture comes to a boil and the sugar has completely dissolved. Allow it to simmer for about 5 minutes until slightly thickened.
    - Remove from heat and stir in the vanilla extract.
7. **Serve**:
    - Once the cake is done, let it cool slightly before cutting into squares.
    - Serve warm with a generous drizzle of toffee sauce on top. For extra indulgence, serve with a scoop of vanilla ice cream or a dollop of whipped cream.
8. **Store**:
    - Store any leftovers in an airtight container in the refrigerator for up to 4 days. Reheat before serving if desired.

Enjoy your Sticky Toffee Pudding Cake with its rich, gooey toffee sauce and moist, flavorful cake—it's a comforting and decadent treat!

Peanut Butter Blossoms

Ingredients:

- **For the Cookies:**
    - 1/2 cup (1 stick) unsalted butter, softened
    - 1/2 cup granulated sugar
    - 1/2 cup packed brown sugar
    - 1/2 cup peanut butter (smooth or crunchy)
    - 1 large egg
    - 1 teaspoon vanilla extract
    - 1 1/2 cups all-purpose flour
    - 1/2 teaspoon baking soda
    - 1/4 teaspoon salt
- **For Rolling:**
    - 1/4 cup granulated sugar
- **For Topping:**
    - 24 Hershey's Kisses or similar chocolate candies (unwrapped)

Instructions:

1. **Preheat Oven**: Preheat your oven to 375°F (190°C). Line a baking sheet with parchment paper or a silicone baking mat.
2. **Cream Butter and Sugars**:
    - In a large bowl, beat the softened butter, granulated sugar, and brown sugar together until light and fluffy.
3. **Add Peanut Butter, Egg, and Vanilla**:
    - Beat in the peanut butter until well combined.
    - Add the egg and vanilla extract, mixing until smooth.
4. **Combine Dry Ingredients**:
    - In a separate bowl, whisk together the flour, baking soda, and salt.
5. **Mix Dry and Wet Ingredients**:
    - Gradually add the dry ingredients to the wet ingredients, mixing until just combined.
6. **Shape the Cookies**:
    - Roll rounded tablespoonfuls of dough into balls. Roll each ball in granulated sugar to coat.
    - Place the dough balls on the prepared baking sheet, spacing them about 2 inches apart.
7. **Bake**:
    - Bake for 8-10 minutes, or until the edges are lightly golden and the centers are just set.
8. **Add Chocolate Kisses**:
    - Remove the cookies from the oven and immediately press a chocolate kiss into the center of each cookie while they are still warm. The cookie should be slightly soft, so the kiss will stick.
9. **Cool**:
    - Allow the cookies to cool on the baking sheet for a few minutes before transferring them to a wire rack to cool completely.
10. **Store**:
    - Store the cookies in an airtight container at room temperature for up to 1 week.

These Peanut Butter Blossoms are a delightful combination of peanut butter and chocolate, making them a perfect treat for any occasion!

Chocolate Chip Peppermint Cookies

Ingredients:

- **For the Cookies:**
    - 1 cup (2 sticks) unsalted butter, softened
    - 1 cup granulated sugar
    - 1 cup packed brown sugar
    - 2 large eggs
    - 1 teaspoon vanilla extract
    - 2 1/4 cups all-purpose flour
    - 1/2 teaspoon baking powder
    - 1/2 teaspoon baking soda
    - 1/2 teaspoon salt
    - 1 cup semi-sweet chocolate chips
    - 1/2 cup crushed peppermint candies (or candy canes), plus extra for garnish (optional)
- **For Garnish (optional):**
    - Extra crushed peppermint candies or candy canes

Instructions:

1. **Preheat Oven**: Preheat your oven to 350°F (175°C). Line baking sheets with parchment paper or silicone baking mats.
2. **Cream Butter and Sugars**:
    - In a large bowl, beat the softened butter, granulated sugar, and brown sugar together until light and fluffy.
3. **Add Eggs and Vanilla**:
    - Beat in the eggs one at a time, mixing well after each addition. Stir in the vanilla extract.
4. **Combine Dry Ingredients**:
    - In a separate bowl, whisk together the flour, baking powder, baking soda, and salt.
5. **Mix Dry and Wet Ingredients**:
    - Gradually add the dry ingredients to the wet ingredients, mixing until just combined.
6. **Fold in Chocolate Chips and Peppermint**:
    - Gently fold in the chocolate chips and crushed peppermint candies until evenly distributed.
7. **Shape the Cookies**:
    - Drop rounded tablespoonfuls of dough onto the prepared baking sheets, spacing them about 2 inches apart. If desired, sprinkle a few extra crushed peppermint candies on top of each cookie before baking.
8. **Bake**:
    - Bake for 10-12 minutes, or until the edges are lightly golden and the centers are set. The cookies will continue to firm up as they cool.
9. **Cool**:
    - Allow the cookies to cool on the baking sheets for a few minutes before transferring them to wire racks to cool completely.
10. **Store**:
    - Store the cookies in an airtight container at room temperature for up to 1 week. They can also be frozen for up to 2 months.

These Chocolate Chip Peppermint Cookies are a delightful holiday treat with a perfect blend of chocolate and mint, making them a favorite for festive gatherings!

Christmas Stollen

Ingredients:

- **For the Dough:**
    - 1/2 cup (120ml) whole milk, warmed
    - 1/4 cup (50g) granulated sugar
    - 1 packet (2 1/4 teaspoons) active dry yeast
    - 1/2 cup (1 stick) unsalted butter, softened
    - 1/4 cup (60ml) orange juice
    - 2 large eggs
    - 1/2 teaspoon ground cinnamon
    - 1/4 teaspoon ground nutmeg
    - 1/4 teaspoon ground cardamom
    - 1/4 teaspoon salt
    - 4 cups (500g) all-purpose flour
    - 1 cup (150g) mixed dried fruit (such as raisins, currants, and chopped dried apricots)
    - 1/2 cup (75g) chopped nuts (such as almonds or walnuts)
    - 1/2 cup (80g) candied citrus peel (optional)
- **For the Filling:**
    - 1/2 cup (120ml) marzipan or almond paste, cut into small pieces
- **For the Topping:**

- 1/4 cup (1/2 stick) unsalted butter, melted
- 1/4 cup (30g) powdered sugar (for dusting)

Instructions:

1. **Prepare the Yeast Mixture:**
   - In a small bowl, dissolve the granulated sugar in the warmed milk. Sprinkle the yeast over the top and let it sit for about 5 minutes, or until frothy.
2. **Mix the Dough:**
   - In a large mixing bowl, combine the yeast mixture, softened butter, orange juice, eggs, cinnamon, nutmeg, cardamom, and salt.
   - Gradually add the flour, mixing until a dough forms. You may need to adjust the flour amount slightly if the dough is too sticky.
3. **Knead the Dough:**
   - Turn the dough out onto a lightly floured surface and knead for about 8-10 minutes, or until smooth and elastic.
4. **Incorporate the Fruits and Nuts:**
   - Knead in the dried fruit, nuts, and candied citrus peel (if using) until evenly distributed throughout the dough.
5. **Let the Dough Rise:**
   - Place the dough in a lightly greased bowl, cover it with a clean cloth, and let it rise in a warm place for about 1 to 1.5 hours, or until doubled in size.
6. **Shape the Stollen:**
   - Once risen, turn the dough out onto a floured surface. Roll or press it into a rectangle about 1/2-inch thick.
   - Place the marzipan or almond paste along the center of the rectangle.
   - Fold the dough over the marzipan, sealing the edges. Shape the dough into a slightly curved loaf.
7. **Second Rise:**
   - Transfer the shaped dough to a parchment-lined baking sheet or a greased loaf pan. Cover and let it rise for another 30-45 minutes, or until slightly puffed.
8. **Bake:**
   - Preheat your oven to 350°F (175°C). Bake the stollen for 30-35 minutes, or until golden brown and a toothpick inserted into the center comes out clean.
9. **Cool and Finish:**
   - Remove the stollen from the oven and brush it with the melted butter while still warm.
   - Let the stollen cool completely on a wire rack.
   - Once cooled, dust with powdered sugar before serving.
10. **Store:**
    - Store the stollen in an airtight container at room temperature. It can also be wrapped tightly in plastic wrap and stored in the refrigerator for up to 2 weeks. The flavor develops and improves after a few days.

Enjoy your homemade Christmas Stollen with a cup of tea or coffee, or as a delightful holiday treat!

www.ingramcontent.com/pod-product-compliance
Lightning Source LLC
LaVergne TN
LVHW081614060526
838201LV00054B/2247